W9-BBO-525

HUMANITY AND DIVINITY

Humanity
and
Divinity

An Essay in Comparative Metaphysics

ELIOT DEUTSCH

UNIVERSITY OF HAWAII PRESS

HONOLULU

1970

BD
111
D45
Cop.2

Library of Congress Catalog Card Number 76-128081
Standard Book Number 87022-190-6
Copyright © 1970 by University of Hawaii Press
MANUFACTURED IN THE UNITED STATES OF AMERICA

TO PEARL AND ALEX

Contents

Preface

Metaphysics, as I use the term, means the articulation of a path to spiritual experience and a disciplined reflection upon that experience. Metaphysics does not mean a *transphysica* speculation that is divorced from actuality (as the term has generally come to be understood); rather, it involves spiritual experience and a systematic interpretation of the contents of experience.

When answering the charge that it would be harmful to practice his metaphysics, Henri Bergson commented that "a principle of explanation is one thing, a maxim of conduct is another." But for a metaphysics based on spiritual experience a "principle of explanation" (a mode of understanding) and a "maxim of conduct" are identical. Metaphysics is a search for, and a study of the implications of, enlightenment.

Now a *search for* does not of course necessarily mean an *attainment of* enlightenment. The philosopher, the metaphysician, does not possess a special occult faculty of seeing (at least there is no reason to believe that he has anything other than quite human capacities of insight and intellect) nor does he have access to a knowledge of facts and causes that is otherwise hidden to science and common sense. He might obtain an enlightenment through the full exercise of his powers of intuition and intellect, and this enlightenment, which is rarely achieved and which one can never claim to have achieved, is indeed held to be wondrous and inexplicable, but it is not thereby "supernatural." A metaphysics is a way of looking *at* as well as *with* the universe that is available to human experience, and the metaphysician must explicitly acknowledge that better ways of looking at and with are possible and likely.

In sum, as I use the term, metaphysics is founded on spiritual experience, on insight into reality, and it is the attempt to understand the world and human existence in the light of that experience. Metaphysics is thus the study of the relations that obtain between human experience and the deepest levels of being—between Humanity and Divinity.

This work is subtitlted "An Essay in Comparative Metaphysics." I see no reason why human experience should be confined to the West. This statement may seem to be so obvious as to be odd. Yet it is certainly the case that most of us in the West are perfectly content to equate human experience with that which is disclosed in Western traditions alone.

By using the term "comparative," however, I do not mean to suggest that I will literally compare or contrast various systems of Western and Eastern metaphysics or try to show similarities and differences between individual thinkers from different traditions—interesting as these comparisons and contrasts might be. Also I do not intend to construct some kind of grand synthesis of world philosophy. Such syntheses usually turn out to be a matter of merely taking a series of ideas from one tradition and verbally harmonizing them with what is apparently contradictory to them in another tradition. I am concerned only with understanding various forms of non-Western experience and with having the thought based upon that experience influence me spontaneously in my own thinking. When contrasts are drawn, when little syntheses are made, they are done so in the service of this somewhat larger comparative end.

It is impossible for me in a work of this sort to express adequately my indebtedness to others, for if this work has any authenticity it will reflect unself-consciously the whole of that formal and informal education so generously given to me by others. Rather than acknowledge the help, advice, and encouragement of specific individuals, therefore, I should like simply to trace briefly the genesis of this book and hope that my appreciation and thanks to others will thereby be apparent.

A draft of this work was completed while I was a graduate student at Columbia University (1956–1959), with parts of it being written during several extended trips to Europe. In 1960–1961, while teaching Western and Asian philosophy at Rensselaer in Troy, New York, a second draft was prepared. Further polishing was done during a research year in India (1963–1964) and during summer research and teaching work at the University of Chicago. The final preparation of the manuscript was carried out in Hawaii during the fall of 1968, and it was submitted to the University of Hawaii Press in January 1969.

PART I

White contains the potential for color. And absolute nothingness is like the whiteness of birth, found again when dying, and what can we, opulent with our venerable logic, know of the actuality of birth and death? Colors incessantly mingle and change, forming infinite varieties within our single substance; continuously moving from one tone, shade, intensity to another: visible combinations and subtle invisible ones for which we have no names. Nothingness is an infinite potential which, when it becomes the content of our human experience, is realized as an absolute completeness; a plenitude in which everything has its being.

The human being is not other than the whiteness and emptiness, and in those moments when it becomes everything it discovers a silence existing beneath its created sounds. Like a cavern with an abysmal depth, the silence draws in and absorbs our feeble words, extinguishing them within its immensity. Then we know that the universe is soundless, that the earth erupts with our moaning symbols; for like the primordial cry of birth, we voice our protestations, creating myths in systems of illusion; describing, expressing in deviating modes of consciousness, multiple visions of the one irreproachable silence.

Death is a concubine to human existence. Living together with our finite selves that are now withdrawn, detached, and suppressed in this the penultimate hour of silence. What is morality compared to the intensity of this inner demand, this inward calling for freedom? A strange and wonderful solitude is feeding on my multiple selves; one by one they atrophy, decay, and fall to the past, leaving me with the bare embryo of my selfhood.

O multiple mask! Fragments of an expanding past! Something within is now purifying my heart, stilling my mind, leading my soul into a terrifying slumber, as though oblivion were the natural home of consciousness. O movements of time, denying the presence of silence, distorting this moment with memories and a thousand dreams!

Suddenly I have lost all status, all labels have fallen from me as from a dead man; I am living in the presence of a divine image. The silence is wonderful and obscure. The once shuddering, vibrating world reaches a point of immobile suspension. Like the fleeting movements of color and light that terminate in twilight, the life-seeds disintegrate, the cord is severed, the links dissolve; I am living on a level of pure existence. A beautiful stillness passes into my soul, transforming my consciousness into Reality. I am alone with an alien truth.

But time still disturbs this imperfect embrace. My self stretches outward and returns again inward; enigma extends back to enigma, back beyond to Mystery itself, further and further, like an endless energetic form constructed of infinite layers; a geometrician's nightmare, a cone which never reaches the point of simplicity.

O eternity! Immortality! Ineffable being! Suddenly in a complete reversion to original form, my superficial self dissolves into absolute nothingness: everything, every event and nascent seed, is seen in this pure stability. The unknown is One, imperishable, complete within the intensity of this timeless moment which reaches a climax in emptiness. Everything is annihilated and thereby becomes. Everything is ameliorated, entering the oneness of being.

Still as I return there is something here, sublime and majestic, infinitely loving, powerful and calm. Something here in this silence, in this nothingness, is joyous and incessantly creates. O man and woman here eternally wed! Something here is destroying, is sustaining, is transforming, O pure order, love absolute, an immeasurable force containing an infinite choice.

A life scream may be heard from the mother's womb. An eagle may be seen rising, circling, preying. Is everything then turned toward death, with death turning into the desire for life?

Silence is the One, creating and absorbing its young.

The Self and the Absolute

From the earliest periods of recorded reflection, and indeed in all sub-sequent ages, man has asked the question Who am I? or What is the self? Further, he has issued time and again that formidable impera-tive, the Delphian inscription, "Know Thyself." It is most often thought that self-knowledge is obtained either through action, through enter-ing into relations with other persons or the things of the universe, or through introspection and self-interrogation which has as its object the solving of some problem, the discovery of some principle related to, or derived from, one's own personality. Goethe sums this up when he writes: "Man knows himself only insofar as he knows the world; he is only aware of either through the other."[1] But man, I would argue, is in essence spiritual. For although he lives as a mental being in physi-cal nature and habitually knows himself only in relational terms, he may experience directly a timeless state of spiritual being wherein he is at-one with his self and with the true self of all beings.

Traditions of spiritual experience in both the East and the West affirm, with unanimity, that beneath our phenomenal self-multiplicity, the plurality that we have formed out of our relations with other per-sons and with Nature, beneath the masks of personality which encom-pass the accidents of our birth, education, and language, our disposi-tions, needs, and capacities, beneath the flux of the "I" and "me," there exists a Self that is pure and timeless, unalloyed and without division, there exists a Self that is entirely free. This Self is featureless and rela-tionless, without category of time or personality. It is not created or conditioned by Nature or society. It is self-caused, or rather it is cause-less; it is beyond all duality and distinction. Though intuitively real-izable, the Self cannot be known as an object of rational knowledge. It can be "known" only in immediate experience.

5

In contrast to the knowledge of our changing self, which expresses the relations of our surface consciousness to our external environment, a true self-knowledge would consist, then, in the realization that man is not at-distance from Reality, but is rather, in his depth, essentially at-one with it.[2]

THE NON-DISTINCTION BETWEEN THE SELF AND THE ABSOLUTE

Although it is not fashionable today to speak of an Absolute, let alone to make it the central focus of a metaphysics or philosophical anthropology, one who chooses to base his reflection upon the depths of experience that are disclosed in different philosophical-religious traditions necessarily has recourse to the term. By the "Absolute" I mean precisely that fullness of reality, that silence pervasive throughout being, which is revealed in spiritual experience. The Absolute for us is simply the oneness of being which is the "content" of the non-dual state of our being realized in immediate experience. It is indefinable as an object, for it cannot be adequately explicated by any series of negations or affirmations. It is not a concept, an object of discursive knowledge, an abstraction from sense experience, or a principle of explanation. The Absolute is rather a plenitude of *presence*. It is a pure indeterminable unity whose abysmal depth is realized only in experience. In experience it is not other than the Self.

When one asks Who am I?, with the "I" referring to one's personal empirical self, one is certain to receive an inadequate answer. Only then does the "I" equal the Absolute—when the small, superficial self of man is as nothing. It is the spiritual self of man, which can never be identified with his physical, mental, volitional, emotional being which is not-different from the Absolute.

The Self, the Absolute, which lies untouched in the deepest recesses of our human being and which is the true self, the essence of all being, may be known, then, only when a many-sided ignorance of ourself ceases. It is our fundamental self-ignorance which causes us to identify ourselves with that which nature and society have created out of us. The immutable "is" of our nature is not to be found in our intellect, in our feelings and emotions, or in our physical being. It is to be found in that silent depth which unites us to the Absolute, to the Divine, to everything.

The Self, the Absolute, is thus a *state of being*.

SELF-EXPERIENCE

What is the way to a realization of Self, to the finding of oneself universally, infinitely? It is within the depth of stillness that the Self may be realized and revealed. It requires a turning inward, a detachment from all outer events and inner happenings so that no thing may intervene between our empirical self and our true Self. The infinite variations, nuances, intricacies, and subtleties of the mind—reason, imagination, memory, will—must be still; attachment to the inviolable dream of this, the finite world of sense, must be obliterated. Concentration must become so intense, so inward and real that it establishes a communion of silence where no distinctions enter. In solitude, in aloneness, the many desires which control our personality and fashion our being must fall to the past, leaving us only with a pure form of selfhood; a form, which, by virtue of its purity, is capable of participating in and becoming one with a supreme Reality.

SELF-KNOWLEDGE AND SYMBOLS

Most philosophers and linguists agree that the meaning of words, as well as their origin, is determined by our human encounter with phenomenal reality; that our languages are constructed of words related to things, relations, actions, feelings, and passions. Due to this relationship of language and empirical existence and to the presence of our separating ego and consciousness, our language of conceptual thought contains an inherent logic and epistemology, both of which are founded on the subject/object, knower/known distinction. Any experience, then, with a noetic dimension which transcends that subject/object situation can only be inadequately expressed, understood, and communicated in our conventional language. With the receding of the habitual functionings of the mind before the deepening of intuitive experience which reveals a reality beyond all distinction, there arises a form of knowing, the contents of which cannot be understood by, or expressed through, the ordinary human understanding. The truth of an Absolute that is beyond all distinction and contingency, though realizable in human experience, cannot be expressed in human words. Language, understanding, and reason always and necessarily recoil before the silent super-conceptual essence of the Godhead.

"Self," "Oneness," "Reality" are words; they are not the content which they symbolize. However, whenever one chooses to communicate, one has recourse only to symbols. Symbols are inwoven with the needs of human nature, and thus they are always limited. They always partly obscure what they seek to reveal. Still, such symbols as "Self," "Oneness," "Reality" do possess meaning for those capable of responding to them. They do perform a function both for those who have experienced the reality which they symbolize and for those who lack that experience: for the one they may provide a means of recollecting experience and of affirming its fruits; for the other they may point to something unknown and inspire a quest to make it known. Symbols in metaphysics are neither "true" nor "false." They are only adequate or inadequate. A metaphysical symbol approximates adequacy to the degree to which it presents the beholder with a means of recollecting or orienting towards that oneness of being that is the Self.

Metaphysical symbols thus cannot exhaust the significance of the experience to which they point. They can, nevertheless, as indicated, communicate in various degrees of adequacy the contents of experience, and hence the meanings set forth by them can be "confirmed" by another person. One has only to look to experience. Self-knowledge does not consist in learning the words "Self" and "knowledge," nor is it attained by referring them to the domain of our ordinary sense-mental experience; it consists rather in *recognizing* their meaning in the ineffable fullness of spiritual being.[3]

The Absolute as Creative-Being

There are, as we have seen, no distinctions in Reality. All distinctions, all separations of subject and object, all differences, dualities, and contradictions arise from a divisive propensity of the human mind and from the practical demands of our experience in the world. All distinctions lack finality. They are applicable at best only to a phenomenal or empirical reality as this is experienced on the level of sense-mental consciousness.

Philosophy, however, survives only where there are distinctions. Thought is utterly consumed, as indeed it is consummated, in the distinctionless abyss of the Absolute. Philosophical thought, which in its customary operation depends upon the existence of distinct objects and a separate self-conscious subject, may serve the truth of the Absolute, then, only in terms of its disclosing the structures which lead away from and which return to it. The Absolute, in other words, cannot properly be made an object of thought; the structures of being as disclosed in many forms of our experience may, however, be discerned—and it is precisely the task of metaphysics to order these structures and to make them available to human consciousness.

But, it might be asked, how in the process of ordering these structures can one avoid reifying the contents of spiritual experience and erroneously conferring an independent ontological status upon them? By its very nature abstract conceptual thought objectifies the contents of any experience that it reflects upon (thought demands a separation of subject and object for its bare functioning), and it thereby radically distorts the content of spiritual experience.

This allegedly necessary hypostatization of thought can, however, be avoided if one confines one's descriptive and analytical efforts to discerning the features and structures of various spiritual experiences, to

tracing the implications of these features and structures for other areas
of thought, and to articulating the relations that obtain between them
and the contents of other forms of experience. Philosophy is not entirely spontaneous. In its role as a systematic exploration of the meaning of experience, metaphysics requires analysis and distinction-making
insight. What philosophy seeks to acquire, nevertheless, in its deepest
dimension, it already possesses; that is to say, it is not the case that
spiritual experience is in itself opaque and is rendered intelligible only
by the force of subsequent analysis; rather, inherent in the experience
is that awakening of the mind that provides the basis for that special
kind of understanding that is of the very essence of philosophy.

Understanding is different from *explaining*. Indeed, in metaphysics,
to explain is precisely not to understand. Spiritual experience always
discloses the complete inappropriateness of any causal explanation of
reality where the criteria of explanation have been established by the
mind in its relations to phenomenal experience alone. For spiritual
experience, Reality is a qualitatively different domain of being and,
accordingly, cannot be accounted for in terms of empirical reasoning
·or explaining.

Metaphysics is not then the ordering of "objective entities"; it is,
rather, the ordering of the contents of spiritual experience, of the structures of being, as these are phenomenologically discerned, in terms of
the actual limitations and possibilities of intellectual understanding.

SUBRATION

To carry out this ordering we need a criterion by which we can make
distinctions between different kinds of being, and the criterion must
clearly include and combine both the valuational and noetic dimensions of our experience. We need, in short, a way by which we may
order the structures of being that are disclosed in experience, according
to the natural dictates of thought and consciousness. This criterion, I
believe, is to be found in that mental process which we may call
"subration."[1]

By "subration" I mean the process whereby we disvalue a previously
valued content of consciousness (an external object, a concept, an existential relationship) because it is "contradicted" by a new experience.
A judgment is contradicted by a new experience when it is impossible
to affirm (to act upon or orient one's attitudes toward) both the pre-

vious judgment and that which is learned or acquired in the new experience.

For example, if one returned home late at night and mistakenly believed that a moving shadow on a wall was that of a burglar, and then later discovered that it had been only the neighbor's cat, one would have rejected one's initial judgment of the object and replaced it with another which, one would believe, conforms with "reality." One would have contradicted one's previous judgment by a new experience.[2]

Subration requires a turning away from, a rejection of, a content of consciousness as initially appraised in the light of a new judgment which takes its place and to which belief is attached. Psychologically, one withdraws one's attention from the content of consciousness as it was originally judged and fastens one's attention either to the same content as reappraised or to another content which replaces the first and upon which a higher value is placed.

Subration thus involves (1) a judgment about some content of consciousness (a physical object, a person, an idea), (2) a recognition, due to another judgment that is incompatible with the initial judgment, that the initial judgment is faulty, and (3) an acceptance of the new judgment as valid.

Subration is a special mental process which involves a revision of judgment. The judging process is not a simple axiological one of the sort "I thought X was good (valuable, important) but then felt that it wasn't," it is rather an *axio-noetic* one of the sort "X, because of a, b, c, is to be rejected and is to be replaced by Y," where X and Y may be any content of consciousness—a concept, an existential relation, a physical object, and so forth. From the viewpoint of the subject, subration is destructive of the object as previously judged; at the time of subration, the object, the content, is no longer capable of eliciting one's interest or of commanding one's attention.[3]

Containing, then, as it does, both axiological and noetic dimensions that are brought together into a functional synthesis, subration is uniquely qualified to serve as a criterion for the making of ontological distinctions. When something is subrated, it is believed by us to have a lesser degree of "reality" than that which takes its place. In terms of subration, our experience dictates that the more something is capable of being subrated the less reality it has, or the more reality something has the less is it capable of being subrated.

APPLICATION TO REALITY

Now the only content of consciousness which cannot in fact and principle be subrated by any other experience, which no other experience
can conceivably contradict, is the experience of pure spiritual identity:
the experience wherein the separation of the self and non-self, of ego
and world, is transcended and pure oneness alone remains. This is the
experience that is celebrated, by everyone who has attained it, as one
of infinite joy and understanding. In spiritual identity the pretensions
to ultimacy of anything else are shattered; in spiritual identity a complete self-knowledge is obtained. What kind of experience could conceivably subrate unqualified identity—the experience of absolute value
where the unique oneness of being stands forth as the sole content of
consciousness?

Subration requires the presence of an object or content of consciousness which can be contradicted by other experience. Reality as non-
dual, in terms of a phenomenology of experience as well as by definition, denies the possibility of there being some other "object" which
could replace it. Just as Spinoza's "substance" cannot be conceived in
terms other than itself, being the whole which includes but transcends
all parts, so Reality cannot be denied by anything drawn from lower
orders of experience. By its nature as oneness, no distinctions can be
applied to it, and all ordinary valuations, which presuppose a distinction between subject and object, must be suspended when confronting
it. By the criterion of subration, then, Reality is that which is when the
subject/object situation is transcended. The Real is that which is the
content of non-dual spiritual experience.

THE HARMONY OF SUBJECT AND OBJECT

There are, though, many forms of spiritual experience, and these experiences disclose different structures of being that can be ordered by
subration. There is the unsubratable experience of undifferentiated
oneness, and there is also the very rich experience in which the
subject/object situation which characterizes our ordinary experience is
harmonized but not fully transcended. A sense of unity, of complete
integration and wholeness is the distinctive quality of this experience.
When the distinction between self and world is harmonized one feels
a natural-spiritual accord between oneself and Reality; one feels an

immense joy of being; one feels oneself to be in the presence of a tremendous power of creativity.

Experientially, the Absolute is here transformed by us into a divine presence. This divinity though is not simply the personal god of the theist, for it is not the converting of a supreme non-personal truth into a personality; rather, the Absolute becomes for us a spiritual structure in which "love," "order," and "will" are in a state of perfect unity. This divine status of the Absolute, in other words, is not a thing, an entity, or an object, it is rather a *state of being* with certain features which may be discerned and which may, symbolically, be expressed. The main features or primary moments of this experience of subject/object harmonization, as disclosed in both Western and Eastern traditions, are "love," "order," and "will."

Love, as experienced in the divine presence, unlike the best of our natural human affection which is so painfully born out of suffering, is love superplenteous and inexhaustible; it is love experienced as wholly present. In this spiritual love, activity and quiescence are grasped as one. Spiritual love is encompassing—it calls for a loving of the love in all beings. This love is experienced, then, not merely as answering to our human need for attention, protection, and care (it is not "personal" love, a communion between lover and beloved in which each retains a radical separativeness), for it is a state of being, a unity, where no "other" is needed. In spiritual love it is felt that all is united in the One.[4]

In the *Bhagavadgītā*, Kṛṣṇa, symbolizing divinity, states that "with a single fragment of Myself I stand supporting the whole universe."[5]

In the experience of subject/object harmony, *order* is discerned as underlying existence and as being pervasive throughout it. In the experience of unity, forms are seen as potentialities, and hence the assertion is made in so many traditions that the Divine is an order containing all forms in *potentia*.

Although the Absolute cannot be confined within any form and is in its essential being free from all form, it encompasses—as a datum or phenomenological feature of unitive spiritual experience—a "logos" principle, a principle of formative order. Like the forces within a flower which express themselves in and constitute its organic structure but which are not confined to that structure, the order of the Divine is experienced as manifest in being and as underlying it as its support.

Order thus becomes the power of the Divine to organize all relations as part of itself. The Absolute, as qualified by the experience of subject/object harmony, is an indeterminable unity wherein all oppositions between subject and object are resolved and contained. 'Order' is thus a metaphysical symbol which refers to the infinite potentiality of the Absolute.[6]

The last primary moment or feature in experience in which the subject/object situation is fully harmonized is that of *will*. In the *Theologia Germanica*, an anonymous work of the fourteenth century, we read: "There is an Eternal Will, which is in God originally and essentially, apart from all works and working, and the same will is in man . . . ." In unitive experience a "volitional energy," a dynamic power which seems not to have any distinct object toward which it is directed, is seen to be present. This energy or power, this "eternal will" is said to desire nothing and to possess everything. In it pure willing and act are one.

The "eternal will," then, is a symbol which points to that aspect of unitive experience wherein ordinary acquisitive desire is overcome and an infinitely greater power of creative force is felt to be present. Neither "good" nor "evil" can be ascribed to it, for it no longer is within that structure of experience where such a distinction holds. The "eternal will" is just that dynamic vital power which is realized in that state of being which is the Divine.[7]

Now this experience of subject/object harmony, or the "qualified non-dualistic" experience as it might be called, cannot by its very nature be subrated by any other experience within the subject/object situation. Although it may be subrated by the experience of utter non-duality, the qualified non-dualistic experience is nevertheless valued commensurate with the fulfillment that it yields. Spiritual love is a consummatory love experience which yields a sense of total satisfaction. No other relational experience is comparable to it. Divine order is also taken by us as complete and necessary. It is like the law of contradiction in logic (which, because of its indispensable function in making propositional truth possible, cannot apparently be denied by a mind that is committed in advance to its use), for once order is present as a feature of spiritual experience there is no other phenomenal content that can stand outside of it so as to contradict it. And similarly with the eternal will: when realized as a feature of experience it provides a sense of immeasurable power; nothing within our ordinary empirical patterns of willing could conceivably contradict it.

The qualified non-dualistic experience, with the features that constitute it, thus stands at that level of being that we take to be "lower" than the Absolute but "higher" than all other experience. Accordingly this level must, from the standpoint of that phenomenal "other experience," be taken by us as creative of all finite being.[8]

LOVE-ORDER-WILL: DIVINE CREATIVITY

One of the oldest recorded cosmogonic myths and one of the most profoundly skeptical statements on our having a knowledge of creation is to be found in the ancient Vedic literature of India. In the *Ṛg Veda* (ca. 1500 B.C.) it is written:

> Who knows for certain? Who shall here declare it?
> Whence was it born, and whence came this creation?
> The gods were born after this world's creation:
> Then who can know from whence it has arisen?
>
> None knoweth whence creation has arisen;
> And whether he has or has not produced it:
> He who surveys it in the highest heaven,
> He only knows, or haply he may know not.[9]

It was for Kant, some thirty-three hundred years later, to demonstrate that rational (or "theological") cosmology is impossible. The human understanding can have knowledge only of phenomena, not of processes that lie beyond the conditions of knowing, processes that are "noumenal." "If in employing the principles of understanding," Kant writes, "we do not merely apply our reason to objects of experience, but venture to extend these principles beyond the limits of experience, there arise *pseudo-rational* doctrines which can neither hope for confirmation in experience nor fear refutation by it."[10] Kant then demonstrates in his famous antinomies that both sides of any rational cosmological thesis can be proved, and hence that all these arguments and doctrines are confined to the workings of reason alone; they do not apply to Reality, for Reality cannot entertain absolutely contradictory truths. Kant thus cleared away the cosmological toil of centuries; but in doing so he limited human experience to the phenomenal. He not only denied the entrance of man's reason into the noumenal, he also denied the efficacy of man's intuitive capacities: he denied, in short, the possibility of spiritual experience.[11]

The limitations which Kant put upon rational cosmology were, I believe, sound; but what Kant failed to see was that "cosmological" statements, which are framed in conceptual terms, may be symbolic statements derived from spiritual experience and that they may be valuable in a systematic reflection upon that experience.

Cosmological speculation for the most part has based itself upon two fundamental assumptions. Along with St. Augustine, it assumes "that the world is, we see; that God [a creative agent] is, we believe [or infer]."[12] In other words, first it assumes the substantiality of the world, that the world possesses an independent reality; second, it assumes that this substantial world necessarily has a cause for its existence, that creativity is essentially a causal process, that the relation that obtains between a "creator" and "creation" is one of cause and effect.[13]

For the present we may put aside the question of the substantiality of the world and concentrate on the problem of the kind of relation that obtains between "creativity" and that which is "created." The Absolute, we have seen, has no object which is essentially separate from itself. Whatever is regarded as deriving from the Absolute, when it is transformed by us into a state of divine creativity, is necessarily an expression of the power of love-order-will: whatever is taken as issuing from the Absolute is the Absolute in a different status of its being. The creativity of the Absolute, in other words, must be conceived of as an ordered deployment of the infinite possibilities of itself. Creativity cannot generate concrete things which are essentially different from their source (this would be in opposition to the very nature of the Absolute); it can bring forth only the structures of which these things may, in their essential nature, represent concentrations. The relation which obtains between the Absolute as creative-being and the Absolute as being, between love-order-will and the structures of existence which issue from it, cannot then be a rational-empirical relation of (material and efficient) cause and effect. Not only is reason impotent to establish a causal relation in creativity (as demonstrated by Kant), but it cannot even conceive of creativity in cause-effect terms simply because creativity and what is created do not occupy the same level of being.[14] We need then a non-causal process relation to understand that experience of what men take to be the creativity of the Divine, and such a relation is that of "conditioning."

"Conditioning," from the active meaning of the term, "to condition," in the context in which I use it, means the imputing of the qualitative essence of one process or state of being into another and without a loss of essence or power of the conditioning agent. The Divine, we must say, imputes its spiritual quality into the structures of being which we take to issue from it and yet, in essence, remains apart from and on a different level of being from these structures. To condition means to *influence*. It means to transmit the qualitative character of essentiality without impairing the integrity of that state of being.

Conditioning, from the passive meaning of the term, "to be conditioned," means then to be influenced by something else, it means to take on the essential quality of a higher state of being. That which follows in our experience from the Absolute as creative-being takes on as its own character the quality of the essentiality intrinsic to the Absolute.

Creativity, therefore, as we understand it, is not a causal process of the sort "given X, Y occurs," nor is it a process which can be explained in terms of specifying a number of necessary and/or sufficient conditions of the kind which we might employ in accounting for an empirical event. It is rather, in phenomenological terms, the continuous process by which one state of being makes itself available to another and which colors and transforms the other without loss to itself.

For man, creativity is frequently a means by which he strives to restore a balance within his nature; it is most often an ordered release from unendurable tensions. For the Divine, the fire of creativity is a self-revelation; it is a harmonious extension of its own being.

Whereas for man, creativity is an act, for the Divine it is a state of being.[15]

In spiritual experience in which the ordinary subject/object situation is harmonized, the Absolute becomes for us a creative power, a timeless unity of love-order-will. From this experiential standpoint, therefore, creativity is affirmed as a status of the Absolute. This creativity, however, is not an "event," for events occur subject to spatial-temporal determinations; nor is it something "physical," as it is entirely a matter of "spiritual energy."[16] Further, it must be stated that when man confronts this creativity, this dynamic love-order-will, alone, he partakes of its sublime power and its illusion. For creativity is illusory if it is taken as separate from its own unfathomable ground, from the pure unutterable being of the distinctionless Absolute. From the standpoint of pure oneness there is no creativity; for there is no distinction between that which conditions and that which is conditioned. Creativity is affirmed only from the standpoint of subject/object harmony. From the standpoint of reason (of separative consciousness) the relation between the dynamic eternal life so affirmed of the Absolute and the structures which follow from it can perhaps best be understood through the language of conditioning. This language seems to conform to the actualities of experience and avoids some of the inadequacies of the usual cause-effect relation.

From the standpoint of subject/object transcendence, then, there is no creativity; from the standpoint of subject/object harmony there is creativity; and from the standpoint of subject/object separation the relation that obtains between creativity and that which is "created" is one of conditioning. Human experience does take place on different levels of being and is necessarily organized from the level of rational-sense consciousness. This being so, any assertion made about a content of experience which is different in kind from the fullness of Reality, from the Absolute, is a "qualified" one; its truth is relative to the experience reflected in it and it is subratable by a higher experience.

The truths of a lower level of being nevertheless do last as long as they are not transcended, and hold logically as long as they are recognized as qualified. Creativity can have no meaning from the standpoint of the Absolute in the fullness of its ineffable being; it does, though, have meaning from the standpoint of that state of being wherein all distinctions between subject and object are harmonized. Creativity, like everything other than the pure oneness of the Absolute, is ultimately "unreal" insofar as it can be subrated by a richer spiritual experience; it is "real" insofar as it is a content of experience and can be affirmed symbolically in conceptual terms. The experience of subject/object harmony, although subratable, is thus not valueless. On the contrary it has an immense value for us both in the immediacy of our human experience and in philosophical reflection on that experience. It discloses an essential spiritual quality in all modes of being, and it also discloses something of great importance to us about ourselves.

THE HUMAN SOUL

Many, if not all, ideas in the history of philosophical thought have undergone considerable change and development; but perhaps nowhere in the history of thought may one find an idea, a term, or concept which, while attempting to refer to something that our immediate experience seems to make impossible for us to deny, is as diverse in meaning as the human "soul." In presystematic thought the concept of "soul" was closely related to the phenomenon of breath. *Ch'i* (Chinese), *pneuma* (Greek), *prāṇa* (Sanskrit)—all expressed this basic awareness of a living, vital principle within man which was taken as a manifestation of a creative power of being.

But it was for Greek philosophy to develop most completely the idea that this life principle was a substance, something that underlies and supports various mental "faculties" and is basically rational in essence. According to Plato, for example, man is "a soul who uses a body." *Nous*, its highest rational part, is that which beholds the eternal Ideas; and for one to attain that rational vision he must learn to separate himself from the lower divisions of the soul, the "spirited" and "appetitive" faculties. Aristotle, who defines the "psyche" somewhat more naturalistically than Plato as the "form of the body," also holds that it contains an "active reason" which is immaterial, imperishable, and hence immortal.

With the possible exception of the Augustinian soul—the living whole of personality which, through self-awareness, is certain of its existence and the reality of God—the classical soul-substance doctrine has dominated Western thought until modern times. The Scholastics, to be sure, refined the doctrine, reconciled it with Christian dogma, and drew out its implications; but nothing radically new was added to it. And to a considerable extent the same can be said for Descartes, Spinoza, and Leibniz. Descartes sundered the soul from Nature—from the *res extensa*, the domain of bodies in motion—and Spinoza and Leibniz sought, in their own ways, to overcome the rigid dualism of Descartes; but it was for eighteenth-century British empiricism to present the first major challenge to the soul-substance doctrine. With its sensationalist-associationist psychology it sought to demonstrate that the soul is nothing more than the sensations which are impressed upon the mind and which, with the aid of memory, are built up into ideas (Hume). Taken in itself as an independent substance or reality, the soul cannot be found or known. Kant carried this idea forward and showed that the traditional concept (or that to which it allegedly pointed) was necessarily outside experience. A substantive unity of self might have to be postulated to make sense out of our experience, but the self as thinking subject can never be an object for itself.[17]

Now, in many respects there is no need to argue with Kant and the classical empiricists' conclusions about the inability of reason to demonstrate the existence of the soul. Like the god of the theist, the soul is not a matter for rational proof or empirical demonstration. But it is arguable whether or not an awareness of a pure love, order, and will embodied within one is closed to human experience.

From the standpoint of the qualified non-dual experience, love, order, and will are seen as features of this experience, and consequently it may be affirmed that the human soul is a manifestation of the Absolute as creative-being: that the soul is a confluence of love, order, and will. In qualified non-dual experience, in which subject and object are harmonized and are brought into a unity, it must be affirmed that the Absolute expresses itself in terms of universal non-personal forces. The soul can then be affirmed as a creative unity manifest in every individual. And when one attains to this "knowledge" of the soul, of the Absolute's status as the Divine manifest in man, it is the universal soul that is "known." One may "know" the soul as it is manifest within oneself but not as it *is* oneself. There is, it seems, no way open to one to affirm an ontological plurality of souls. The creative action of the Divine is not that of a splitting up of itself into separate parts. The soul is simply that which is realized as an eternal presence of love-order-will in an individual's experience.[18]

Ideals of Man: A Critique

Ideals, like ideas, are not mere fanciful dreams. For just as each individual creates and possesses one or more images of himself—projections, as it were, of the life roles which he elects to play—and subsequently, through his experience, through repetition and habit, he tends to become a stereotype of that experience, so man as a thinker and creator as well as an actor is always, to a certain extent, formed by the conception he possesses of himself as a man and the ideal which he puts forward as his highest possible nature. Between the "classic man" and the "classical view of man," between the "Christian man" and the "Christian view of man," there exist definite, though not always easily discernible, correlation, interplay, and mutual influence. A man both creates and is created by his knowledge, understanding, and ideal of himself as a man.

A survey of the history of man's formative ideals of himself reveals that the basis on which they are constructed include at least these two general considerations: (1) the conception he has of the nature of the universe and environment in which he lives; and (2) the selection of some one or more aspects of his nature—either as a guiding principle or as one which, through a belief in its larger possibilities, is felt to deserve a more extensive or exclusive development—and the subsequent relating of this aspect to those features of his life and universe which he conceives as of greatest importance.

In the West three views of man's nature stand out as being most representative of this formation of self-ideals and their consequent formative effect upon him. These are the "natural view," the "rational view," and the "paradoxical view" of man. Almost all influential Western philosophies of man may be subsumed under these forms or may be viewed as representing a combination of them.[1]

THE NATURAL VIEW

According to the natural view of man, as expressed in "scientific" or "critical" naturalism,[2] the functions of the human mind have assumed their distinctive character as a result of explicit purposes; they have developed in each individual according to the dictates of specific necessities. Reason, the imagination, the intricate processes of perception and conception, all the habitual functions exist because they are necessary. They operate contextually in patterns directly related to the exigencies of adaptive behavior. Any act of the mind, according to the critical naturalist, necessarily occurs in Nature; any claim to a spiritual self-transcendence is delusory. A discriminating, practical, analytic intelligence is thus taken as man's most adequate instrument for obtaining knowledge and happiness. Everything about man is explainable, at least in principle, and in terms which do not extend beyond "scientific" intelligence. Man is the most complex being that has evolved out of the potentialities of Nature, and his perfection consists in the mastery, use, and enjoyment of his natural environment. Man's world is pluralistic. He is involved in mental processes, biological functions, and environmental contexts which, by their limiting nature, prevent him from entering into any form of relation with a transcendent Divinity and, by incessantly immersing him in the relative, prevent him from realizing immanently any unconditional state of his being.

But the moment a man is aware of possessing an inner life which, by its very nature, can never properly be an *object* of another man's explanatory inquiry, scientific naturalism—as a total view of man—is refuted. It is recognized as spiritually naïve. When a man enters into an abyss of solitude, when he feels the need for transformation in the presence of an overwhelming spiritual silence, when he meets with the bare fact of his limited self and sees it as a deformation rather than an expression of truth, such a man has gone beyond what scientific naturalism can tell him about himself. He knows that the depth of his being is incommunicable; he knows that he possesses a life untouched by the exigencies of practical necessities; he knows with the deepest certainty that his selfhood which can be explained lacks ultimacy.

A man cannot be adequately *explained* as a thing among other things, as just another event in a universe of blind processes, rather he can be *understood* as a person only in his fundamental relations with spiritual being, that is, in his own essential nature. His "intelligence," whether taken individually or collectively, may enable him to solve problems which would otherwise inhibit his smooth functioning in society (although the entire course of human history seems to show that even this limited claim stands in need of considerable qualification), but his intelligence also quite clearly binds him to a ceaseless adjustment to an ever-changing "environment." It does not set him free.

The formative effect of the scientific natural view of man, one must conclude, has been to limit man's nature. Although for some the acceptance of this view has brought about an increased ability to control and order the environment and to be liberated from narrow dogmatism and superstition, it is nevertheless the case that when a man believes that he is wholly conditioned by his relations with physical nature and other men, he becomes incapable of seeking, let alone of finding, the freedom of his essential being. He believes that the common ground of mankind is to be found only in the fact that each man is subject to the same natural laws, possesses the same rights, and lives in the same world. But this sameness is bondage. It would keep us forever on a surface consciousness; it would not release the full potentialities of our human being. By making a philosophical virtue out of what he takes to be a biological necessity, the scientific naturalist simply misses the central spiritual dimension of man.

The scientific naturalist sees man as a combination of determinable functions adjusting to and controlling his environment; the "romantic naturalist," on the other hand, sees man primarily as a will-full being, as a creature endowed with an immense drive for self-development. According to the romantic naturalistic view, man is primarily a historical creature: an understanding of him requires the seeing of him as a being striving in time for greater self-enhancement.

Romantic naturalism thus approaches man and his life through his "instincts" and "passions" as these are exhibited in an evolutionary development in Nature. Man is the "bridge leading nowhere," according to Nietzsche, and his essence is a "will to power." Man simply deludes himself when thinking that through his mind he is able to exercise a central control over himself. It is only the *Übermensch* who is able to control himself and the world through a creative expansion of his will. Reason itself then in the last analysis is only a tool for "rationalizing" the results of various unconscious drives and instinctual motivations.

But the true nature of our will is not to be found in an exaggerated self-consciousness, in the "unconscious," or in an animal vitality. It is to be found in the depth of the soul. It is in the "eternal will" that the real power of vitality resides. Man, essentially, is not a mere combative dualism of intellect and will; he is in a fundamental harmony, for order and will, together with love, are his eternal becoming.

According to Bergson, our intellects are incapable of bringing us into contact with the stuff of our true reality. "Intuition," which is according to him opposed to reason, and not a complement of it, alone accomplishes this. For intuition is a "means of possessing a reality absolutely, instead of knowing it relatively, of placing oneself within it instead of adapting points of view toward it...."[3] And further: "There is at least one reality which we all seize from within by intuition and not by simple analysis. It is our own person in its flowing through time, the self which endures."[4] But this self which endures is itself, according to Bergson, insubstantial; it is pure *durée*. It is without purpose and leads nowhere; in other words, it is purely "romantic."

In the depth of man's being there is no time; hence, on the essential level of his being, man has no history. Man is free to choose history as he is free to accept or reject as inclusive that part of him which contains and binds him to history, namely, his memory, intellect, and imagination. History, when taken as an ultimate truth, is a myth. History is only appearance; it does not pertain to Reality. The Self, the Absolute, does not evolve; only man evolves in his experience of and living through it.

In recognizing the inadequacy of all purely intellectual interpretations of life, that life cannot be grasped by the categories of science alone, the romantic naturalist does free men's feelings and emotions from servitude to biological needs and allows them to assume a cognitive and truth-revealing role. The romantic yearns for a universe in sympathy with human ideals, and he discovers that the universe does indeed possess ample scope for the full play of his diverse energies. He demands that men keep close to experience, that their abstract constructions ought not to extend beyond their capacity to feel. Although romantic naturalism (especially in its *Sturm und Drang* variety) with its not infrequent *Weltschmerz* and cult of the genius readily passes into the morbid, the wayward, the irresponsible, it nevertheless compels man to recognize those sides of his nature which he too often conveniently puts aside. Romantic naturalism thus brings man back to his vital sources and infuses fresh values into his life. It will arise as a formidable force whenever there is a too facile *Aufklärung* (enlightenment) which places an unwarranted trust in the reasonableness of life and of human nature, and which emphasizes an artificial culture. As a critique of a one-sided rationalism or scientism, romantic naturalism is refreshing; as a solution to the human condition, as a formative view of man, it is manifestly inadequate.

THE RATIONAL VIEW

The next view of man which we briefly take up has been criticized perhaps more than any other in recent times, but it has nevertheless continued to maintain a tenacious hold upon the mind of man. This is the "rational view" of man. According to it, the distinctive characteristic of man's nature is his reason. Aristotle's *nous*, the Stoic's incarnate *logos*, Descartes' "mind of clear and distinct ideas," Hegel's *Geist*—all embody this same basic principle: man's differentia is his reason, his capacity to order experience, his power to discern the intelligible structure of nature, to make judgments between objects, to make inferences from observed facts, and to make deductions from general principles. Reason is that which separates man from the rest of Nature and unites individual men together. We understand ourselves, according to the rational view, in terms of our having a common capacity and power of reason. And we understand ourselves only as we are in an ordered world, be it a purposive cosmos, a non-purposive, mechanical universe which follows fixed, immutable laws, or an organic whole which unfolds itself through its own historical contradictions. Man, then, according to the rational view, is superior to this world as he stands outside of it as its explainer; he is inferior to it as he is but one of its parts. Still, he is a whole unto himself. However otherwise rational views of man disagree among themselves, there is unanimity in this, that man is a species of a very special kind. He stands at the dividing line between gravity and mystery and is not wholly comprehensible in terms of either.

The primary supposition of the rational view of man is that the "logic of thought," in whatever way it is specifically formulated, is identical with the "logic of reality." But the Absolute transcends all logical formulation, and thus man, who bears within himself a representation of all spiritual principles, can never be understood as though he were essentially a rational being. Reason is indeed a characteristic capacity of human nature; it is present, with greater or less efficacy, in all individuals, but it is not the essential content of that nature. Man is rational, and he is something infinitely more; and, being infinite, that "something more" cannot be identified with a finite reason. By surpassing the limitations to self-knowledge which follow from a sole reliance upon reason, we may attain to a knowledge of our self as participating in, and being at-one with, an infinite richness of being. We cannot, then, be defined adequately according to our reason—which, by a curious irony, usually ends in our being defined according to our ignorance; we can be understood only as we are beings who are capable of surpassing and transforming our empirical self and finitude.[5]

Reason cannot be identified with our essential nature, and further it is incapable of bringing us into an intimate relation with it. Reason has its own proper and restricted sphere of activity, namely, the controlling of our lower impulsive nature and the dealing with rational structures in Nature; it is, however, unable to grasp the nuances and subtleties of the life-process of man, or the non-rational, non-personal, transcendent level of essential reality. Our essential nature is free from all forms, relations, and categories: reason functions only in forms, in multiplicity; our essential nature is one.

The effect of the rational view of man, insofar as it has been held by men, has been to restrict and to divide his nature. It restricts him by giving him a false security in a finite power; it divides him by making of him a rigid separation between rationality and animality. In short, the rational view of man prevents man from affirming the totality of his being.

THE PARADOXICAL VIEW

According to Pascal, man cannot be reduced to the natural or the rational. Possessing the ability to attain consciousnes of his anomalous place in existence, obsessed with yearnings and aspirations for the Divine, fearing yet desiring the presence of God within him, man is the great contradiction and paradox. He is a divided being, alone and frightened in the vast and silent spaces of the universe; he is sublime and wretched, strong and without real power, he is knowable to himself only through an unknowable mystery. His heart has reasons of its own which engender a faith to which the intellect must assent—and this through a "wager." *Qu'est ce qu'un homme dans l'infini?* is the great existential question posed by Pascal. Its answer, or rather the basis of the question, having been given to him in certain ecstatic moments when "fire" and the "God of Abraham, Isaac, and Jacob" replaced the artificial god of the philosophers. Man is a thinker, and "thinking reed"; and as an existing being he is the supreme paradox.

The last view of man which we shall consider is the "paradoxical view." It finds its fullest expression, I believe, in Existentialism and in Protestant Christianity.

In spite of the fact that "Existentialism is not a philosophy but a label for several widely different revolts against traditional philosophy,"[6] to the student of this revolt, certain definite outlines of a philosophy of man appear to be present. Man is a being who lives by the dread of choice and is constantly threatened by Nothingness. Still he has the potential to live an "authentic existence" which transcends any form of circumscribed being, and he has an essential freedom which is actualized in concrete "engagement." In Kierkegaard (1813–1855) we have one of the clearest expressions of this view or attitude. No account of Existentialism omits him, and indeed he is most often considered to be the father of this revolt against traditional philosophy.

According to Kierkegaard, "truth is subjectivity." Truth is not just a quality of a concept of proposition, it does not belong exclusively to that which can be agreed upon publicly, rather it is a quality of one's own being. Truth is an inwardly appropriated, passional state[7]—it is a name for a special type of reflection and for a special state of one's whole being. Kierkegaard puts it this way: "*An objective uncertainty held fast in an appropriation-process of the most passionate inwardness is the truth,* the highest truth attainable for an *existing* individual."[8] Kierkegaard thus argues that genuine thought, "existential reflection," requires having the full awareness of oneself as an existing subject, and for him this means the cognitive awareness of oneself as existing in the presence of God.

This reflection, this awareness, demands choice and decision—the choosing of oneself as a self in relation to God. Thus, "God is a subject and exists only for subjectivity." But the faith that emerges from this relationship is entirely paradoxical. Faith demands that the individual *qua* individual "enter into an absolute relation with the Absolute."[9] One must recognize oneself as a being in the presence of God and at the same time acknowledge oneself as a finite individual; one must consent to the distance that separates infinite love from finite individuality. If one were to surrender oneself wholly to the unseen other, one would lose one's individuality, the status of being a "single one" which alone permits one to be real.

Throughout his life Kierkegaard, it seems, was bound in tension between his awareness of himself as an exceptional individual and his acceptance of the Christian doctrine of love, with its notion of an equality of worth obtaining between individuals. In his posthumously published "That Individual: Two Notes Concerning My Work as an Author," Kierkegaard distinguishes between "the individual" and "the crowd." "The individual" is one who is open to all persons as individuals and thereby accords them equal honor; "the crowd" is the untruth that a man is his function and status in society, his objectivity rather than his personhood is honored. Each man thus is truly "the individual." But, as Kierkegaard paradoxically puts it: "... He [God], the great Examiner, says that only one attains the goal. That means, every one can and every one should be this *one*—but only one attains the goal."

In the thought of Martin Heidegger (of the *Sein und Zeit* period) we find the idea that man is "thrown into being." He exists without a predetermined nature or *raison d'être*. The essence of his being in the world is that he discover something to do, that he have a "care" (*Sorge*). Still, as a finite being, man incessantly falls from his proper environment (the world as a whole) into the complex ambiguities of the human world. Caught up in this world in his state of fallen-ness (*Verfallenheit*), man senses his transiency and becomes aware of his inevitable death. A man's mood (*Stimmung*) thus penetrates and colors his entire world, with anxiety (*Angst*, the threat of nothingness, the awareness of radical finitude) being the primary mood.

It is with Jean-Paul Sartre, though, that we find Existentialism presented in its most striking and controversial form. The basic question that he raises is, What kind of a being is man who becomes a man of *mauvaise foi* (bad faith)? And his startling answer to it is that man is a "useless passion."[10]

Starting from Descartes' *cogito*, Sartre distinguishes between two kinds of being, *l'être-en-soi* (being-in-itself) and *l'être-pour-soi* (being-for-itself), between the being of mere objects or objective phenomena and the being of human consciousness. But consciousness, we discover, is throughout social in character: "I cannot obtain any truth whatsoever about myself, except through the mediation of another." And yet at the same time "To be conscious of another means to be conscious of what one is not," for "Consciousness is a being, the nature of which is to be conscious of the nothingness of its being."

"To be," for Sartre, means "to be free"—to be without a pre-given human nature. Man, however, ceaselessly engages in activities that drive him to *mauvaise foi*, to bad faith or to self-deception; he ceaselessly turns himself into an object, *l'être-en-soi*, and thereby hides from himself the reality of his freedom.

For Sartre, a man is defined by his deeds. A man has no essential potentiality; he is his actuality and his actuality is "particular." God alone can have a "universal" consciousness; but there is no God and so "there is no human nature because there is no God."

Man is not comprehensible to himself then, according to Existentialism, when he makes of himself a mere object of inquiry or when he sees himself in relation to an Absolute. He understands himself rather only through an efficacious inwardness. It is when one encounters one's own subjectivity in the light (or darkness) of immediate existential experience that it is possible to attain an adequate idea of one's being. "Communication" between man and man is thus a serious problem. Man is unable to communicate adequately the truth of his existential situation to another and hence bears the pain of being grossly misunderstood.[11]

Existentialism has made a substantial contribution to philosophy in its demand that philosophical problems, to be significant, must be lived. It has concentrated attention upon individuality and has rescued it from the oblivion to which it was cast by Hegel's idealist followers. A man is not something "objective," to be treated as a mere part of a rational system or as a statistic, rather, he is an inner-life, a person. Existentialism, however, misses the truth of individuality which it is bent upon attaining for the simple reason that man possesses true individuality, true personality, only in the Infinite. Man realizes his true *Existenz* only when he becomes a "universal-I," only when he overcomes the distinction between "I" and "not-I." The apocalyptic biographical insight of existential enlightenment allegedly gives one a knowledge of the meaning (or lack of meaning) in life. A more significant enlightenment, however, would give one the knowledge not of oneself as a separate being but as united essentially to the oneness of Being.[12]

By turning the Western philosophical tradition upside down, as it were, especially as that tradition is grounded in Greek ontology and Judaeo-Christian values, Existentialism has revealed some primary weaknesses in Western philosophical anthropology. The most important of these perhaps is the idea, handed down in modern times from Descartes, that it is through an objectifying self-consciousness that one grasps the essential quality of human being. Existentialism properly criticizes the objectifying pole of consciousness, when this is taken in isolation, but by turning to the opposite pole, the subjective, it tends only to plunge man deeper in ignorance. For it is when consciousness is turned toward the Infinite and becomes unself-conscious that man attains to his true being and essence. It is when one becomes conscious of the eternal life of love-order-will which underlies the surface flow of one's differentiated self-experience, of true personality behind the ego, of the Self with its pure conscious existence, of the undifferentiated oneness of being, that one knows oneself in one's essential being and one's self as spiritually united to all other beings.

According to Judaeo-Christian revelation,[13] man is a "creature." He is begotten, he is called into existence by the Creator. Man and his world are "real," for the Creator creates nothing "unreal"; man and his world are essentially "good," for God creates nothing "evil." But man, according to Christianity, is also a miserable creature simply because he is a created being; he is unable to attain independence, he is fragile, pitiable, even contemptible. A yawning distinction exists between God, the Creator, and man, the creature created in His image. Creatureliness is man's essence. Evil is centered in his will, in his unwillingness to acknowledge his status—his dependent being.

A man is essentially a sinful and a suffering creature. According to St. Paul, sinfulness belongs to man's elemental nature, to his flesh, and it belongs to man universally. It is only when the transforming power of the Divine spirit intervenes that sin is overcome. St. Augustine, differentiating between "the good and bad angels," writes: "And if we ask the cause of the misery of the bad, it occurs to us, and not unreasonably, that they are miserable because they have forsaken Him who supremely is, and have turned to themselves who have no such essence. And this vice, what else is it called than pride? For 'pride is the beginning of sin.' They are unwilling, then, to preserve their strength for God; and as adherence to God was the condition of their enjoying an ampler being, they diminished it by preferring themselves to him."[14] Wicked flesh and pride comprise, according to Pauline-Augustinian

Christianity, the two sides to sin. But, as a famous Buddhist text puts it: "All that we are is the result of what we have thought; it is founded on our thoughts, it is made up of our thoughts."[15] And, in the *Gītā*: "A man is made by his belief, as he believes so he is."[16]

Historically it appears that any revival of the Pauline-Augustinian theology—with respect to that portion of its doctrine which views man as the sinner, as the fallen creature who must undergo conversion, and not through his own efforts so much as through divine grace, in order to overcome his radical alienation from a personal god—is based upon man's discovery that he is ill-equipped to master his existence. He feels inadequacies within himself which he takes to be ultimate. He transforms these feelings into doctrines of ontological separativeness, sin, and dependency. But man cannot look upon himself as essentially evil and upon the Divine as good, without at the same time denying the Divine. For, as St. Paul himself states: "He therefore that despiseth, despiseth not man, but God who hath also given unto us his holy Spirit."[17]

According to Ludwig Feuerbach, an unsympathetic critic of Christianity: "The Christian religion is the religion of suffering. The images of the crucified one which we still meet with in all churches, represent not the Saviour, but only the crucified, the suffering Christ. Even the self-crucifixions among the Christians are, psychologically, a deep-rooted consequence of their religious views."[18] But, according to Meister Eckhart, "suffering is the fleetest beast to carry one to the perfect."

Suffering may purify or destroy. Suffering which is brought about through one's relations with other men or with physical nature, as these are taken in isolation from the Divine, may leave scars and deformation; suffering which occurs by virtue of one's relations to the Divine may yield beauty and re-formation.

This religious suffering is not an ultimate imposed upon human nature. Man's capacity to suffer is almost without limit, yet suffering forms no part of man's nature, which is unlimited—for there, there is love. And then we read: "The love which enters history as suffering love, must remain suffering love in history.... Love must continue to be suffering love rather than triumphant love."[19] But the idea of a "suffering God" is an objectification of a simple and crude fact. Christ allegedly took all human misery, inequity, and pain, all suffering upon himself in order to free men from it and to redeem them. But it is man, the unregenerate, objectifying, natural man, who imposed suffering on Christ. Love is indeed triumphant love. In the depth of love, in the soul, there is no suffering, there is only power and joy. Love triumphs over all pain, all disintegration, misery, and inequity; for love, without category of time, is the Divine.

Christianity, we read, "rightly regards itself as a religion, not so much of man's search for God, in the process of which he may make himself God; but as a religion of revelation in which a holy and loving God is revealed to man as the source and end of all finite existence against whom the self-will of man is shattered and his pride abased."[20] And also that "Christianity cannot admit the possibility of a coincidence, even partial, between the human substance and the Divine Substance. For the Christian God is Being—*ergo sum qui sum*—and this creative being is radically other than the Being of his creatures."[21] But according to Jesus: "I and my father are one."

The central question, and for us perhaps the most important theological problem, of Christianity is, Does the "I" here refer to Jesus the man, or to man's essential being?

Naturalism holds that a man is entirely conditioned by Nature and that a knowledge of this constitutes intellectual enlightenment. Christian theology holds that there was an enlightened man who was at once conditioned and unconditioned and that this is a supreme mystery and paradox—a belief in which is necessary to salvation. But all men in their true essence are at-one with the unconditioned, and a direct realization of this means spiritual enlightenment.

The Divine, the Absolute, in its own pure being is indeed other to the actual mental-emotional-vital complex of human nature, to the unregenerate "I" of personality (and indeed to church militant), but it is not other to the essential nature of man. There are no distinctions in spirit. The Incarnation is a perpetual, timeless process. It is an everlasting bringing forth of essential being, of divinity. Each man ideally then is the Messiah. Each man must be his own intermediary to perfection, to the realization of that timeless, unconditional state of his being that is divine.

PART II

Out of the silence, out of the permeating quietude, the child's first song transforms the stillness into a world of sound—holding there something strange, wonderful, and complete—as when we, extending our mind and heart into the universe, envision a delicate order, a perfecting beauty out of everything that lies within our mediate concern.

There is within this union of intellect and feeling a subtle logic which, unlike other habits of the mind that correspond with each attempt of the head to impose itself upon Nature, creates a harmony rather than a rupture between self and that which self acknowledges to be infinite.

It is as though this mode of feeling-thought were perfectly assimilated to a hidden logic within the structure of being; as though the self were a child playing according to some primordial rule of life; and yet there is something deeper here, more beautiful, like the innocence of the wise.

My self is pure, intense, and whole. Free from the chains of self-awareness, desire dissolves into love, free from the longing for possession.

There is a love relieved of acquisitive desire; a sustained not a fragmented intermittent love that is buried deep within and which is brought to the surface and developed in solitude.

There is a beauty in this love, a silent enduring beauty entirely different from the intoxication known in the sea of emotion; here the beauty, the love, is sufficient to itself; requiring, anticipating nothing, completely contained, it therefore spreads itself out to encompass world.

The Absolute as Being

THE ABSOLUTE AND EXISTENCE

In an earlier section on creativity we saw that the relation that obtains between the Absolute as creative-being (*natura naturans*) and that which follows from it (*natura naturata*) is, from the standpoint of intellectual understanding, one of conditioning. Love-order-will, we must then say, conditions the structures which constitute being. "Existence" is throughout immersed in the spiritual; all the structures of being that we recognize must be seen to issue from, to be conditioned by, the spiritual power of love-order-will.

The Absolute, then, from the perspective of intellect, has as the object of its creativity itself in another status of its being. For us the Absolute as creative-being gives rise to the Absolute as being. The Absolute, in other words, must be seen as "existence" in one of its modes of being.

To affirm the Absolute as being is not, however, to assert that the Absolute is reducible to a concept of being; rather it is to assert that "being" is one of the primal ontological levels which may become a content of our experience. The Absolute, from the standpoint of spiritual experience, at once assumes being and transcends it.[1] It is the task of metaphysics to study this assumption of being by the Absolute and to disclose, as far as that is possible, the basic structures that constitute being. Further, it must ask, How does man, who is at once essential and existential, interrelate with these fundamental structures?

THE CATEGORIES

In order to set forth the structures of being and to interpret human experience, philosophy, throughout its history, has made use of various categories. The meaning that has been attached to categories and the implications derived from them, as well as their very enumeration, have however differed widely.

Plato, for example, from his belief that "there is more reality in the motionless than in the moving," conceived of categories "realistically" as objective features of the world which correspond to certain *a priori* or innate ideas in the mind—for example, mathematical concepts and logical notions such as identity and difference, unity and plurality—in other words, to those realities which correspond to intellectual definitions of objects other than those given directly in sense-experience. Categories, according to Plato, possess an ontological and a logical status. All men have the same fundamental categories, for all men are essentially rational.

Aristotle, on the other hand, who may be taken here as typical of the naturalistic tradition, conceived of categories in several senses: (1) as principles of the understanding which correspond to the various forms of things; (2) as terms which signify the modes of being of the things themselves (e.g., something is a substance, a quantity, a quality); and (3) as terms which represent a grammatical classification of various forms of speech.

In contrast to "realism" and "naturalism," Kant viewed categories strictly as *a priori* forms of man's sensibility and understanding. They subsist without any necessary reference to the actual contents within the world of sense-experience; that is, they are applicable to, but are not derived from, whatever man does experience. In his "transcendental aesthetic," Kant presents the forms of space and time; in the "transcendental logic," the categories of thought as they are derived from a classification of logical judgments. By an inward necessity of the mind these pure concepts of the understanding are translated into the active terms of temporal consciousness and, as "schematized," are applied to perceived objects. The categories do not apply to things as they are in themselves, to the noumenal world of reality, but only to phenomenal nature. The categories, then, are constitutive of nature, for nature is simply phenomena viewed under the laws and forms of the human understanding. The categories are at once independent of experience and are the conditions for the unity of experience.[2]

A strictly "realistic" conception of the status of categories misses the truth about the structures of being and of human nature as it places undue emphasis upon the logical and transcendent nature of categories, and it fails to recognize adequately their presence in sense-

experience; it fails, that is, to grasp the dynamic character of our experience by regarding categories as fixed, unchanging, logical forms.
A strictly "idealistic" interpretation, on the other hand, misses the objective side of the categories of being when, as in Kant, it emphasizes
their subjective presence in man. It is unable thereby to set forth or
posit sensibly the interrelatedness of man and nature.³ Both the
"realistic" and "idealistic" orientations lose sight of, or purposively
neglect, the individual side of human experience. They implicitly assume that experience is the same for all men. Naturalism (insofar as
it is grounded in empiricism and recognizes the individual) avoids this
mistake but tends to lose, on the other hand, all that realism and
idealism have gained. It is not able to encompass what is truly universal in man's interrelation with nature and, confined as it is to sense-
experience as the basis of all experience, it is never able to meet with or
comprehend the essential level within which all experience is grounded.

By "categories" I mean those basic features of being (of human consciousness as it finds itself in intimate relation to the Absolute as
being) which are operative as structural features of experience for all
men and which assume qualitative and quantitative determinations in
individual experience. The ontological status of a category in this organization is threefold: the categories of being are *subsistent*, they are
beyond empirical determination; they are *existent*, they are generic
features of consciousness or human being; and they are *developmental*,
they are specific contents of experience. The categories are at once
essential, universal, and *individual.*

This threefold division of human experience is demanded by the
nature of experience: it takes into account the fact that there are three
fundamental directions of consciousness (sensual, intellectual, spiritual)
and that human experience is related to an essential order of being,
is part of a universal structure, and is individualized.

A category in its *subsistent* dimension represents a feature or content
of consciousness as consciousness realizes the Absolute as being. It is
thus a feature of being that is beyond determination (that is, cannot
be determined in terms of empirical experience). A category in its
existent dimension, on the other hand, is a structural feature of all experience and is determinable as a universal presence in mental life.
Whether a category here is to be thought of epistemologically as *a
priori* or as derived from experience is quite irrelevant to the purpose
of defining its ontological status. A category in this its second level,

status is assuredly not *a priori* in the sense that it compels the mind to accept the truth of some proposition, or that it gives rise to the necessity or certainty of some truth, or that it is a necessary condition for or presupposition of scientific knowledge; nor is a category empirical in the sense that it can be traced back to some kind of elementary sense-data and, accordingly, be reduced to its origin. Ontologically, in its *existent* status, a category is simply a recognizable organizing capacity or feature of consciousness in its intentional state of relationship with what is taken as external to it. Whatever we experience in the domain of sense-mental consciousness is experienced as categorically structured or interpreted. The categories are not static forms which are merely imposed by the mind upon an otherwise "buzzing confusion," rather in their status as organizing forms the categories assume innumerable contents and are altered thereby. A category, and now in its *developmental* status, becomes the content that it embraces; it becomes individual, specific; it becomes the state of consciousness of someone as categorically described.

Experience, on the empirical level, is thus viewed at once in universal and individual terms and as it is grounded in the essential order of being. Empirically the categories function as anticipations of, and consequently as guides to, experience. Through the categories the mind is brought into intimate contact with an "objective" world. We each move about in this world for the most part in an unself-conscious habitual way so that it becomes quite impossible for us to distinguish ourselves from the content of our consciousness. We become our experience by becoming bound to our habits of seeing, interpreting, and acting. In fact, the alteration in the shape, as it were, of a category in its existent status takes place according to the interests of activity which it serves—interests which are peculiar to each of us. But this does not mean that individual consciousness is capriciously "subjective" or atomically "personal." "My" present state of consciousness, at any given now, is already deeply social. My habits of seeing, of interpreting and acting are grounded in the exigencies of living in a particular environment (cultural, historical, as well as geographical), and this particular environment is assuredly not created by me or even for the most part freely chosen by me. (No one has a choice about the time or place in which he is born.) Still it is the case that at any given time my consciousness is never identical in content with that of another. My peculiarities of seeing, of interpreting—my particular choices of objects or ideas to attend to—are always present and give a unique color and quality, a special style, to my experience.

Whenever a category is asserted then it means that it can be seen as a feature of the Absolute as being, as a generic trait of consciousness, and as it is present in the intricacies and subtleties of our individual experience. Three dimensions or sub-levels are included at once in the assertion of a category. And the same word which designates the category must be used at all levels. The same word, however, is not adequate to apply to different orders of experience as this could involve a simple equivocation in terms. A word which may apply adequately to phenomenal experience may be applied only by analogy to non-sensuous, non-rational levels of being. The word, however, is never the thing. The difficulty of using language on several levels at once can be diminished if one is aware that they are merely names for realities and assume a different quality as they move from a naming of things which are apparent to ordinary experience, to a naming of processes which are available only to certain types of efficacious philosophical experience. The deepest level which will be investigated here is the Absolute as being. All categorical language which is applied to it is only and necessarily symbolic. Although in most cases the meaning of categories, in this their deepest level, will be expressed by referring them to that level of experience that is closest at hand to us, I do not mean that their application to other levels is a mere extension from that more ordinary experience; rather, I mean that categorical language is genuinely symbolic in the sense that the realities to which it refers on the deeper level are in fact first in order of value. Rather than being an imaginative extension from sense-experience, the realities are themselves experiential and alone properly illuminate ordinary experience.

The categories which will be set forth are categories of "feeling," of "mind," and of "understanding." The distinction between "feeling," "mind," and "understanding" is not meant to split the structure of being into disparate or conflicting parts, rather, it is intended only to differentiate various types of categories and enable us to see these types according to their relative conditioning efficacy.

Philosophers are so accustomed to think of categories as only conceptual (i.e., as forms of understanding or intellect) that it no doubt appears somewhat strange to talk about categories of feeling. But to restrict categorical interpretation to abstract mental life does seem arbitrary. If a category of being is an aspect of experience that is evidenced in and is constitutive of all experience, then for metaphysics "feeling" is as important as conceptual understanding—and indeed, in at least one dimension, is more important. The categories of feeling are the basic features of that subtle domain of emotive life that goes to condition all activities of mind and consciousness. They are the structural features of various states of feeling being. The categories of mind, on the other hand, are the generic (psychic) features of consciousness that make for a dynamic, integrated conscious being. They are rooted in feeling and themselves condition those formal (epistemic) principles of consciousness that we call the categories of understanding. The categories of understanding are forms in terms of which consciousness is cognitive, whether in states of reason or intuition.

The following is a list of the categories which will be examined briefly in their multi-leveled ontological status:

THE CATEGORIES

Of Feeling	Of Mind	Of Understanding
rhythm	purpose	space-time
proportion	memory	relation
integrity	the ideal	universal
	equilibrium	causality
	continuity	

Categories of Being

Love-order-will expresses itself as pure feeling. For us, feeling is every-where present in being, for it is a *presence* to be found everywhere in being.

It is difficult, if not impossible, to set forth with exactitude the con-stituent elements of feeling; for whenever we experience a feeling presence we are aware primarily of a flow and wholeness of vital being. Upon reflection, though, certain factors or dimensions, certain categories, stand out as prominent.

Rhythm

Wherever there is life, there is rhythm. The uterus at birth, flowers, trees, laboring bodies, songs, and the sea—each has a rhythm natural to itself, and each reflects the pure rhythm pervasive throughout being.

From the standpoint of intellectual understanding, the Absolute manifests itself within being as one of its statuses, rhythm is every-where present in being; it is part of the structure within the move-ment, the becoming of the Absolute. Just as the form in a work of art is not simply the formal arrangement or collocation of the elements which constitute it, but is rather a subtle unity which expresses dis-ciplined formative energies, so the rhythm pervasive throughout being is not a mere formal quantitative sequence, a dull recurrent balance of systole and diastole, but is rather a formative inner-controlled energy, a dynamic qualitative potency to which the movement of all else in the universe, in varying degrees of intensity, bears a discernible relation.[1]

The primal status of rhythm is a timeless subsistent. It is a presence without beginning or end. It expresses itself, however, in innumerable ways. Everything in nature has rhythm, and within the human mind and heart there is a subtle rhythm, a spiritual feeling that can be violated only with injury to the individual being.[2]

This inward rhythm of man is a universal existent. It is an embodiment, as it were, of the pure rhythm subsistent in being. The realization of this rhythm in an infinite play of spiritual feelings yields joy. The realization of this rhythm is a recognition of its intrinsic at-onement with the pure rhythm of being.

The rhythmic stirring which the poet feels just prior to and throughout his creativity, the special rhythmic motions which, when discovered, enable one to perform some physical task with grace and pleasure—all reflect the basic truth that the life of spirit possesses a rhythm and spiritual life is a life in harmony with it.

Rhythm is a category of feeling. It subsists as a content of experience in its own pure being, it is manifest universally, and it is particularized in individual experience. All rhythms which we meet with in ordinary experience are related to a universal rhythm, even if they are a distortion of its purity and are, if they are expressions of that purity, grounded in the essential rhythm intrinsic to being. To recognize a rhythm one must become like-hearted to it. One can recognize only that which is akin to oneself.

Rhythm is thus an expression of spiritual vitality and possesses the dignity of a primary category by virtue of its conditioning potency. Everything in life is in part determined by the rhythm native to it. Every living thing has its nature in terms of the way rhythm manifests itself within it.

Proportion

St. Thomas Aquinas writes:

... Beauty relates to a cognitive power, for those things are said to be beautiful which please when seen. Hence beauty consists in due proportion, for the senses delight in things duly proportioned ....[3]

"Proportion," as illustrated by Thomas, is most often conceived as a formal relation that obtains between the elements which comprise a whole and as that which (among other things) gives beauty to the whole; the relation being apprehended through the senses and affording delight to the mind.[4] Like "rhythm," though, "proportion" can be conceived as belonging preeminently to the order of feeling. "Proportion" may be seen as a pure quality resident in being, as universally present in human being, and as subject to an unlimited individual expression.

As a category of feeling, proportion is not a quantitative relationship of one part to another or of one part to the whole; it is a qualitative relation between a whole and that which it meets. For feeling is always whole and, in its relational acts, establishes an appropriateness, a fitness between itself and that which it encounters. Feeling, however, is not determined by its object; it is "non-intentional," it has no need of an object in order to be.

Further, when in a feeling state—when knowing ourselves to be in consanguinity with a feeling energy present in being—we are aware of an integration, a harmony within ourselves. And this integration, this feeling of harmony is experienced as a "gestalt," as a state of being with qualities greater than any mere summation of parts. This means that the harmony experienced is not simply one which results through parts—it is not an integration of, or harmony between something—but is *sui generis*, it has a wholeness native to itself. And yet, like any "gestalt," it is not completely independent; there is an internal relation between the harmony and the elements which make it up, and this internal relation is also what we mean by proportion as a constituent of feeling. It is that which gives order to feeling. "Proportion" is the name, then, for those aspects of feeling that structure the meeting between a feeling state and any object and that structure the internal energies of that state into a dynamic whole.

Integrity

Integrity is that within being which gives to it its self-sufficiency. Integrity, in other words, is that constituent of being which enables being to support itself as an integral whole. Integrity is that formative energy, that spiritual power and presence, which gives wholeness to being.

"Proportion" is the name for the relational structuring of feeling; "integrity" (and the term is used here apart from any special moral connotations) is the name for the very quality of wholeness that characterizes feeling. And like rhythm and proportion, it is universally manifest in all systems of nature and gives to these systems their capacity for qualitative wholeness. Integrity, in its native purity, is present in human nature and is a fundamental link between our essential life and our outward becoming in time. Without integrity, our being would be an unrelated disjointed dualism of our essential nature and our actual existence. But our life is a whole and is intimately related to the whole, to the oneness of being. Integrity is also manifest in all qualitative organizations in nature. A work of art, a sunset, even a gesture may exhibit integrity. Anything that we experience that has a spiritual wholeness, necessarily has integrity.[5]

THE CATEGORIES OF MIND

The processes of the human mind, we are now aware, are highly dependent upon feeling. The meaning and significance that we give to concepts, to things, to other persons is deeply colored by our state of feeling. The very power of one's intellect is grounded to a considerable extent in feeling, for if the feeling (the "commitment") be weak and ill-developed, so ultimately will be the thought.[6]

The categories of feeling are basic structural features of experience in its feeling mode. The categories of mind are generic (psychic) features of consciousness. They are necessary conditions for the functioning of an integrated consciousness and their presence is, accordingly, necessary for the functioning of cognitive consciousness.

Purpose

Consciousness, in its pure form, is a power of awareness subsisting in being. It is an infinite and unified awareness. Nothing is excluded from its embrace, and no thing *qua* thing—i.e., no separate independent thing—is included. Consciousness in this its pure form is a vision of wholeness, of totality, of oneness.

"Purpose" in the Absolute is thus "purposeless purpose." It is a feature of that state of being in which there is no attachment, no interest or attention to anything other than to itself. In that calm serene awakening that is symbolized as the Absolute as being there is nothing that is wanted, there is nothing toward which consciousness is directed that is alien to itself. Purpose in the absolute consciousness is diffused equally throughout being and never ceases to be unitary and whole.

Our human consciousness is at once intimately related to this unified vision, capable as it is of its realization, and is a distortion of it. Human consciousness in its everyday half-awakened state is purposive: it seeks objects to attend to, to relate with, to appropriate.[7] To have a purpose means to have an end in view. It means to direct action according to a preconceived or immediately discerned end. We are purposive when we act with concentration and selectivity; we are purposive when we accept some ends and reject others. Whenever a conscious being sees anything, thinks of anything, imagines anything, "purpose" is present in consciousness. Purpose thus gives to our everyday consciousness its directiveness. It enables us to concentrate the otherwise disparate energies of our awareness onto that which is (we assume) other to ourselves and to fasten, as it were, our being to them.[8]

The category of purpose, then, has for us an existent status in consciousness, and it is also actuated in our individual experience in many and diverse ways. Specific ends are sometimes achieved by us and new ones chosen, or they are sometimes rejected before achievement in favor of others, and so on. "Purpose" is thus a feature of the Absolute as being, it is a generic feature of our consciousness, and it has a developmental status for each of us.

Memory

According to Aristotle, "all memory implies a time elapsed; consequently only those animals which perceive time remember ...."[9] And Plotinus writes: "Now a being rooted in unchanging identity cannot entertain memory, since it has not and never had a state differing from any previous state ...."[10] The Absolute as being, then, is without "memory." Past, future, and present are to it as one. That state of being which is the Absolute as being possesses the consciousness of holding all things in itself, simultaneously, as a unity, as an unchanging identity. All events are present to the Absolute essentially; no events are reviewed by it actually. It is in this sense, then, that the Absolute as being can be said to be a "fullness of memory."

And man, in spite of the fact that he is one of Aristotle's animals who perceives events in time, is essentially not-different from the Absolute. For man has the capacity to attain to the state of the "fullness of memory" by becoming one in consciousness with the Absolute as an unchanging identity.

The state of the "fullness of memory" and the state of "memory in time" are, however, incompatible. For, as St. John of the Cross expresses it, "if the soul pays attention and heed to the apprehensions of the memory—seeing that it can attend to but one thing at a time—and busies itself with things that can be apprehended, such as the knowledge of the memory, it is not possible for it to be free to attend to the incomprehensible, which is God."[11] What then is the ontological relation that obtains between the memory that is "outside of time" and memory which is bound-up in time? What is the ontological status of memory?[12]

As a category of mind, memory is multi-leveled. In its primal status it is a subsistent power of being: the power of retaining all in the consciousness of oneness. In spiritual experience there is no ordinary memory, no recalling of events with emotional colorings or identifying of what has been learned in past experience; in spiritual experience one is aware only of the coincidence, whether partial or complete, between the human and the Divine—that is, one is aware only of the fullness of being.[13] In its second-level status, memory is a universal feature of consciousness—one which acts as a necessary condition for the ordered workings of consciousness. All conscious beings possess memory, the capacity to link temporal experience together into meaningful gestalts, and this capacity, when activated, directly intrudes upon and is present within all conscious states and actions. In our ordinary sense-mental consciousness memory is an inescapable presence.

The third-level status of memory is that with which we are most familiar. It is the multi-faceted functioning of memory in our ordinary waking consciousness. This third-level status of memory is its developmental status. Memory assumes a multitude of forms, embraces innumerable contents, and makes at once for an integrated and immeasurably diversified human experience. No single thinker can do justice to the subtleties and intricacies of memory, and no thinker ought to overlook the fact of those subtleties as a basic status of memory. These subtleties enter into all of our perceptual and conceptual processes, into all acts of our sense-mental consciousness.[14]

In sum, memory is a *category* of the mind because of its being a generic (psychic) feature of consciousness. It is one of the dynamic principles of, and necessary conditions for, an integrated consciousness. In spiritual experience, however, there is no memory in the usual sense of the term, as there are no outer events or inner changes in consciousness to attend to. Nevertheless consciousness of the Absolute is not an annulment of ordinary consciousness, it is not a void, rather, it is the fullness of awareness and accordingly represents a fullness of memory —the retaining of all in the Absolute as being. In its second-level status, however, the category of memory is the linking together of empirical experience into meaningful wholes; its presence is a precondition for all cognitive and creative activity. Memory is here a universal feature of consciousness. But memory is not merely an abstract or formal feature, instead, each of us has his own memories and at any given moment incorporates memories in a special way into the intricate pattern of experience. Categorically, then, memory has its subsistent, its existent, and its developmental status.

The Ideal

In the Absolute the ideal is the real. Any addition to the being of the Absolute would only be a subtraction from what already is.

"The ideal" as present in human consciousness is that which permits us to know the finite as imperfect and relative. The category of the ideal as manifest in mind enables us to move from "what is" to "what ought to be" in actuality.

The ideal is a generic feature of consciousness and its presence can be discerned in all sense-mental experience.

To assert the ideal as a category is not to assert the necessary existence of some one or more particular ideals; rather, it is to assert the necessary presence of a capacity for ideality in consciousness. This capacity is clearly recognizable, as it is the very source of the discontent which usually accompanies consciousness. We are aware of the distance that separates some given actuality from the ideal which we envision for it. And this discontent, which is a natural consequent of the presence of the ideal in consciousness, is itself a source for much of the creative change that we impose upon our life and culture. Human consciousness is most often divided and in anguish by virtue of the call of the ideal within it.

The existence of the ideal as a category of mind was largely a discovery of Greek culture. Greek philosophy attached a superior moral status to excellence. It gave rise to the idealization of classical art, the abstracting and generalizing from individuals in order to represent the perfect type suggested by, but not embodied in, those individuals. And this idealization for the Greek was not so much an artistic convention or style as it was a genuine realization of the actual existence of the ideal as a human capacity. The purer the mind, the greater its excellence, the more apparent is the ideal to and within it. Being awake to the ideal possibilities of things was for the Greek a sign of maturity. It was a triumph of the mind over crude sensation.

But what the Greeks did not see was that the ideal is a multi-leveled category of mind and that the usual ideal-forming capacity of the human mind is perhaps a distortion of the real character and meaning of this category.

The ideal, in its subsistent status, is not something wholly fixed and at rest; it is, on the contrary, an expression of an unlimited, dynamic freedom. Further, as incarnate in man, the ideal need not present a definite limited boundary to his action and being; it can present him with the opportunity for seeking an unlimited experience; it can provide him with a stimulus for making of life a dynamic spiritual adventure.[15]

It has been said that all sense-mental experience contains an element of ideality within it. Do we ever see or think of anything apart from valuational processes? Do we not each express an intrinsic and ever-developing system of values? Idealization and criticism necessarily involve each other. And every moment of perception is bound up with criticism. We do not see things simply as they are, as they have their being, but as they are selected by us and are related to our valuations of them. For our sense-mental consciousness, if everything were equal nothing could be recognized in an habitual, friendly way. The "ideal" must then be seen as a subsistent feature of being, as having an existent status in consciousness, and as developmental.

Equilibrium

Equilibrium is the concentration of, and perfect balance between, the potentialities latent in being. It is a dynamic state of wholeness.

Our common notion of equilibrium it seems is based upon two conceptions: the Greek idea of harmony and the mechanist's idea of balance. Equilibrium to the Greeks (e.g., Plato) meant the creating of a harmony between the disparate and opposing forces within one's nature so that one could act in a wholesome unity. It was the healer of the otherwise irreconcilable tendencies which divided one's being. It was, then, something artificial, that is to say, something contrived. Equilibrium was not intended to be a direct reflection of a process already present in being, rather it was to be a construction of the intellect, a reign of the mind over the lower forces of nature that threatened it. For man, however, a true equilibrium is one that does reflect the equilibrium resident in being. Whereas an artificial equilibrium is always liable to disintegrate, to give way to the assertion of one or more forces over it, a genuine equilibrium can never be other than it is. Once established, no disharmony or disorder can affect it. A state of equilibrium thus transcends all conflicting elements and is not a product of them. It does not result from merely settling the disputes within oneself but is something *sui generis*, it has its own proper activity and status in being.

Whereas the Greeks looked upon equilibrium as essentially a harmonizing of forces, physical (mechanical) theory regards it as a balancing of forces. It is that state of a given body which by its nature is free to move but is so acted upon by external forces (through their directions and magnitudes) that the body can no longer move. Equilibrium is simply the resultant of physical forces and disappears the moment these forces are such as to permit the body to move. It is this strictly mechanistic conception of equilibrium which we perhaps most often associate with the term and extend to other forms of discourse. In aesthetics, for example, we read that "balance is based on equilibrium, on the meeting and neutralization of opposites, on deadlock and stabilization. Development is based on disequilibrium, on the transformation of opposites into directional movement ...."[16]

Both the Greek and the mechanist conceptions are thus capable of being disrupted. For both, equilibrium ceases to exist the moment there is a disharmony or inbalance in the elements or forces which constitute it. But a man is fundamentally integrated within himself. In the center of his being he is a concentration of potentialities that are in accord with each other. Equilibrium, although seldom realized in actuality, is an integration of energies. It is the source of that dynamic poise and serenity of being that we can meet within ourselves and others.

And an integration of energies is, from the standpoint of understanding, that which our relative experience strives to attain. For us, a generic feature of our experience is just this quest for dynamic stability. Sense-mental experience is a changing experience and, on the subjective side, it moves, as it were, from an initial discharge of energy to an integration of energy.[17]

Further, this quest for and movement towards equilibrium is individuated in experience. Each of us works toward a somewhat different kind of equilibrium, faced as each of us is with somewhat different external conditions and internal energies.

Equilibrium thus becomes a multi-leveled category of being. It subsists as a harmonizing of the potentialities of being, it exists as manifest within us at the core of our own being, and it is present for us as a developmental feature of all experience.

Continuity
Henri Bergson writes:

> Just as we separate in space, we fix in time. The intellect is not made to think *evolution*, in the proper sense of the word—that is to say, the continuity of a change that is pure mobility.... The intellect represents *becoming* as a series of states, each of which is homogeneous with itself and consequently does not change.[18]

Continuity, for Bergson, is thus the essence of an undivided transition, of an indivisible mobility. Bergson tends to regard the continuity of change as that which is ultimately simple, and he thereby confounds the essence of "becoming" with being itself. "Continuity," we would maintain, is a multi-leveled category of mind: it is a subsistent character of being, a universal feature of consciousness, and a developmental form manifest in all experience.

As a subsistent character of being, continuity is simply the timeless becoming of the Absolute as being.[19] The Absolute is continuous with itself; it is never modified by something outside itself.

And man is contiguous, as it were, with the Absolute. Continuity is present in our being and is the form according to which we persist in time. Except in moments of morbidity, consciousness is continuous: there is that within it which, in spite of its successive attentiveness, its incessant dispersion throughout phenomenal existence, gives to it a coherence and consistency in the fundamental modes of its functioning. We identify ourselves, in fact, as persons by the continuity of our mental processes.

Continuity, then, as disclosed in its existent and developmental statuses, is that principle of dynamic being which structures a process so as to bring *consistency* to it. "Consistency" means several things: logically, a statement or argument is said to be consistent when it is not necessarily false, or a set of axioms is said to be consistent when it is impossible to derive both a theorem and its negation from it (or if not every formula in the logistic system is a theorem); psychologically, a series of inner states is said to be consistent when the observable behavior associated with these states follows a pattern which does not inhibit the attaining of the goals toward which the action is directed. Consistency here does not rule out novel changes, it does not suggest a mechanical routine of which every aspect is predictable; rather, it means the binding together of changes in such a way as to yield a "whole" action. To be inconsistent would mean to be a series of activities which are at cross purposes with one another. The core meaning of consistency then which underlies both its psychological and logical uses is simply lack of contradiction.

In terms of human experience this continuity, this consistency, serves both a negative and positive function. Negatively, it makes for a restricted response to experience, the refusal to admit or to deal with forces that would, if recognized, call for a radical change or break with oneself. The demand for continuity in sense-mental experience brings about a withdrawal from the challenge of novel experience in order to retain one's self as is. Positively, however, continuity makes for the channeling of energies in an efficient way; it makes possible the carrying through of an action to its completion.

As a subsistent character of being, continuity is the essence of an undivided becoming. In its existent and developmental statuses, it makes for an integration of change and for the structuring of experience in a consistent way.

THE CATEGORIES OF UNDERSTANDING

"Purpose," "memory," "the ideal," "equilibrium," and "continuity" are categories of mind. "Space-time," "relation," "universal," and "causality" are categories of understanding. By "categories of understanding" I mean structural principles or formal characteristics of being and of our cognitive consciousness. Our mental life is viewed here in metaphysical terms as consisting in acts of consciousness that are categorically structured. And I use the term "understanding" not in order to suggest a Kantian type of distinction between *Verstand* and *Vernunft*, which is used basically to articulate areas of legitimate rational inquiry, but to make clear that my concern is with the status of our mental life in being. My purpose, in short, is not to inquire into the structure of the mind in order to determine how we think or how we acquire knowledge (I make no claim to proffer an explanation of things or an adequate description of psychological/epistemological processes); my sole concern here is to trace some of the implications that follow from the axionoetic fact of the Absolute as being as it is a content of human experience.

Like the categories of feeling and mind, the categories of understanding possess a threefold ontological status: they are *subsistent*, they are features of being beyond specific determination; they are *existent*, they are manifest in man in their native purity as generic forms of his mental being; and they are *developmental*, they are actuated with varying degrees of intensity in all experience and they assume a multitude of relative contents. Our consciousness is in intimate relation to the Absolute as being, and it has its universal and developmental character.

Space-time

The ignorant live in the present, the learned in the past and future, the wise in the eternal Now where all is contained.

Our ordinary awareness of time is dependent upon our consciousness of events. For human consciousness, where there are no events there is no time. This "void" from which we incessantly flee, however, is not eternity. Eternity is neither a mere denial of a beginning or end nor an indefinite extension of ordinary serial time; it is rather the manner of existence of spiritual being. The Absolute as being is a fullness of time and is an undivided presence.

Physical distance is measured psychologically by time (i.e., the time it takes to traverse the distance). In the eternal, in the Absolute, consciousness is at once "everywhere" and "nowhere." Hence the conjunction of space and time as a category of being.

Plotinus asks: "How can we come into contact with things that are foreign to us? It is necessary, therefore, that we should participate of eternity. Since, however we exist in time [and space] how is this possible?"[20] Kant answers negatively. "Space," he writes, "is nothing but the form of all appearances of outer sense. It is the subjective condition of sensibility, under which alone outer intuition is possible for us." "Time is nothing but the form of inner sense, that is, of the intuition of ourselves and of our inner state."[21]

But "time" is clearly not so much a condition of knowledge, a form of sense-intuition, as it is a feature of being, a content of experience in terms of which we have our being. And time, for us, is necessarily a multi-leveled feature of being. We do indeed participate in the fullness of time, in eternity, for eternity is a fact of experience, and we can experience only what is akin to ourselves. A consciousness of events is also a fact of our experience, for we have an awareness of a "durational" time, and we fill our capacity for time and space with innumerable contents.

Each stage of our consciousness thus has its own corresponding sense of space-time. Ordinarily our consciousness is a disjointed spreading out, a dispersion of its power over a wide and complex field of events. It is, however, possible to withdraw consciousness away from the many attractions and events of the empirical field and back to its original source and primal status. To get "outside of time and space" means simply to transcend that form of consciousness in which we bind ourselves to transient events and to attain to a higher form of consciousness in which ordinary time and space are not, and eternity alone is.[22]

Customarily, as indicated, our awareness of space-time is never separate from our awareness of events. And this awareness of events is *anticipatory*. We constantly anticipate events within a sequence; we seldom, if ever, become aware of an event in its singularity, that is, in total isolation from other events. Psychologically, our ordinary experience of spaces-and-times is as a series of gestalts. We experience a duration of spaces-and-times in "wholes" which are more than the sum of their respective parts. We live in a sequence of events, and not with a sum of isolated events. It is this unifying aspect of consciousness which reflects the existent status of space-time, and it is these varying sequences that determine the developmental form of space-time as a feature present in all experience. Unification is a contribution of consciousness to experience. It is the actuation, as it were, of the existent status of space-time present in the understanding.[23]

In human experience there are many kinds of space-time determinations. Our awareness of space-time is always relative to our interests and modes of attention.[24] The naïve idea of space as a receptacle of transient contents is not the same idea of space as formulated in science—whether it be Newton's absolutistic framework of space and time, or the modern notion of relativistic, multi-dimensional continuums (with all spatial-temporal determinations being made relative to some frame of reference or "definitional system"). Space to an architect is not the same as space to a painter. Subjectively, there is a rich diversity of times-and-spaces. Time, we say, sometimes moves slowly, as when we are waiting for someone, on other occasions, quickly, as when we are absorbed in some pleasant task. There are "vacuous moments" and there are "dramatic moments." Every moment of perception is bound up with various types of judgments, needs, interests, and purposive selectivities which always influence our spatial-temporal awareness, and which themselves incessantly change and undergo alteration. Space-time within our consciousness clearly admits of variations. It is actuated in different individuals in different ways. It assumes different forms as it combines with natural sensory data and events.

Our ordinary commonsense idea of space-time as something within which bodies move, as a context for external events measurable by clocks and rulers, is thus but a convention. It is interesting to observe, however, that for our ordinary existence it is a necessary convention. It gives stability to our phenomenal experience. It can only be more or less, but not completely, dispensed with in ordinary consciousness.[25]

But that which is a necessity to our ordinary intellectual consciousness does not necessarily exhaust a truth of being. In fact, our ordinary awareness of, and need for, an external order of sequential space-time does not include that most fundamental truth of space-time as an indivisible simultaneity, a fullness without parts. For spiritual consciousness there is only eternity.[26] This leads me to mention briefly a problem that confronts all notions of space-time, the problem of the meaning and status of history.

We are aware that events in ordinary space-time influence one another but that they never touch the eternal. In the Absolute there is no sequential space-time and consequently there is no history. It follows that history, when taken as an independent ultimate, is a myth. History has only a relative status; that is, it has a status relative to and dependent upon our own human consciousness.

Events hurl themselves into the distance and disappear. The fullness of space-time remains.

In sum, any philosophical schema which seeks to understand time and space must incorporate the special space-time qualities that are present in all the basic forms of experience. In spiritual experience, in experience of the Absolute (and here in its status as being) one recognizes a space-time quality to be present in and to consciousness, which is different, in significant ways, from space-time qualities which we recognize in our ordinary empirical experience. In spiritual experience consciousness knows nothing of a quantitative succession of moments or of a pattern of qualitative reactions to them; it recognizes only a "present" which is indivisible. Space-time is interpreted then as a plenitude and as a form of our understanding. In the latter dimension it operates durationally in all acts of sense-mental consciousness. One cannot think abstractly except in temporal terms, that is to say, in succession; one cannot cognize events except through temporal-spatial orderings. Space-time is thus multi-dimensional: it has its subsistent character, its existent manifestation, and its developmental function.[27]

Relation

The Absolute is a unity in which the essences of all things are present. The Absolute as being is a *coincidentia oppositorum*, a unity that embraces and transcends all opposites and contraries. "Relation," in this its highest status, is just this unity of multiplicity, this coincidence of all things in the Divine.

"Relation" has its own subsistent character which is beyond conceptual determination; "relation" is also incarnate in man as a form of his understanding and it is present in all his sense-mental experience.

For the most part philosophy has recognized only the lower status of relation and has given to this status only a formal character. According to the idealistic doctrine of "internal relations," for example, nothing has a nature independent or separate from its relations to other things. Everything is interrelated with everything else; each thing is determined by its relations with other things. Fichte expresses it thus:

In every moment of her duration Nature is a connected whole; in every moment each individual part must be what it is, because all the others are what they are, and you could not remove a grain of sand from its place without thereby, although imperceptible to you, changing something throughout all parts of the immeasurable whole.[28]

In short: "everything that exists in the universe needs the universe as a whole as a necessary condition for its existence ...."[29]

But is the doctrine of "internal relations" a description of Nature or a transference of the inner necessities of reason to Nature? In questioning Nature one indeed discovers that no thing can be understood (ideally) apart from everything else; that one needs to take into account all remote as well as proximate causes for the full explanation of some happening; but this does not itself establish the fact that everything in Nature is so interrelated. A necessity of reason is not the same thing as the structure of Nature. Along with its doctrine of "internal relations," objective idealism asserts that the real is the rational. But the real is not the rational, and the interrelatedness of things is not the result of a rigid necessity in Nature. Things, persons, processes are, to be sure, when taken empirically, determined in a very real way by their relations to other things, persons, and processes. One's phenomenal or empirical self is, in fact, to a considerable extent precisely the result of its relations. A man is very much a different person by virtue of his "fatherhood"; "friendship" is not a neutral abstraction that one passes in and out of, for one is changed by one's friends; and so on. But these are existential facts, not a logical structure of Nature. Ontologically there remains a unique dimension to persons that is untouched by empirical relational experience.

We are able nevertheless to recognize something *qua* thing only if we see it in relation to something else. Mathematics, logic, and hence the sciences would be impossible if everything were approached as if it were wholly individual and unique. Relation, then, is a generic feature of our cognitive consciousness; for us it is a means whereby we interpret things.

Further, in our actual experience "relation" embraces many varied contents. Our mental lives, rather than being uniform, are diversified. In our individual understandings we portion off various aspects of being for attention and analysis; different minds will thus always discern different relations. At any moment each of us, insofar as we are involved in a state of cognitive consciousness, is awake to a complex of relations that is special to ourselves, the complex being largely a matter of our own choosing.

Relation is thus a multi-leveled category. In its subsistent status it is that within the unity of being whereby all essences are present. In the Absolute as being, relation is the *interpenetration* of all things. In its existent status the category points to that condition of our consciousness by means of which we order events by the establishing of connections between them. Developmentally it points to the presence of these connections in all individual sense-mental experience.

Universal

The universal is the crossroads of relation. A universal has reality because of the common relation particulars have to the essential. "Man" is not a mere collection of men, rather, man exists as a reality because all men are determined in their nature by their relation to the Absolute.

Universals exist because the Absolute subsists. Universals are real because the essential is the Real.

My contention here is that once one recognizes the Absolute as subsistent being, one can assert the reality of universals (that the objects
of thought signified by class names, and so forth, have an ontological
grounding) on the basis that the particulars that come under the universal can be seen to have common relations to the Absolute—relations
which determine the being of the particular. Thinkers for whom there
is no Absolute tend to hold that particulars alone exist: that "men"
exist with certain shared qualities and capacities, but that "man" is
post rem, a mere abstraction.[30]

The traditional concern with the "problem of universals" rests, however, on several mistakes. It asks what the relation is between the particular and the universal as though such a relation could be specified
without reference to an essential order of being, and it assumes frequently that the universal is itself a kind of particular (especially in
Plato's universals or Ideas as archetypal entities) and thus renders unintelligible the whole question of the status of universals. The traditional concern fails, in short, to comprehend the category of the universal as it has a necessary threefold status in our experience.

In its first-level status as a feature of the Absolute as being, the
universal must represent the totality of possible relatedness. In the
Absolute the relations between it and everything that is taken as other
than its own pure being are resumed. The primal status of the category of the universal, then, is simply that of its subsistence as the
nexus of the relations of all things to the Absolute.

In its second-level status the category of the universal is precisely
that feature of consciousness which, among other factors, enables us to
identify objects as particulars. The category functions here as a condition for the coherence of experience. This is borne out by the recognition that in our sense-mental experience the universal is clearly as
much an object of experience as is the particular, that in fact we see
things initially not so much as they possess special or unique qualities
but as they represent various combinations of universals. Ordinarily,
we see things as topical instead of as individual. (Hence the difficulty
and indeed rarity of seeing things in a fresh "aesthetic" way that demands that we see things precisely as individual and unique.) In our
ordinary perception-conception, universals overlap. For example, when
we look at a tree we see it at once as something generic, as it has properties in common with other trees and as it has properties that distinguish it from other types of things. We look at a tree in terms of a

complex of universals, and only then do we see it as an individual thing. We cannot even recognize the particular as such without the presence of universals, for we would have nothing with which to raise the particular from a crude sensation to a meaningful precept. In our sense-mental experience universals are productive, as it were, of particulars.

This leads to the third-level status of the category of the universal, which is its developmental actuation in experience. The capacity to discern universals is operative throughout our sense experience and in an individual way—i.e., we each, at any given time, discern universals that are special to ourselves. We are interested in, we look for, we see different things.

Causality

In the Absolute there are no successive states of time and, hence, in the Absolute there is no determinable cause-effect structure. The Absolute is *causa sui*, is purely self-caused; it is beyond the antithesis of freedom and necessity. Still the Absolute is the matrix of the order of all manifested being and is, in that ontological sense, the source of all causal relations in being.

Causality, then, as applied to the structure of being means something other than that "an occurrence is causally determined if it can be predicted with certainty,"[31] for no mind can predict events within the Absolute as being, simply because there are no events as such there to be predicted. Causality, in this its first level status as a category, must ultimately mean non-rational conditioning. The Absolute is the "ground," everything else is its "consequence."[32]

Causality has long been recognized as the universal principle of change. It is a distinctive human way of perceiving phenomena, and our experience seems to demand that it is a presence in Nature by which events are organized.[33] Causality is manifest in human consciousness as a power to discern the causal structure in Nature, and it is present as a "force" operative, as it were, upon other aspects of human nature. Man, existentially, is bound up with time and is subject to causal complexes. The "unconscious" levels of our psyche constantly intrude upon our conscious processes; our physical nature is constantly subject to, and directly reflects, the various emotional and mental states of our being. Man partially represents causation.[34] He also possesses the capacity to discern causation, and in that sense, at least, he is superior to it. If Nature is a complex network of causal relations then the human mind exceeds Nature insofar as it is able to view Nature as an independent object. The less one is involved in a causal order the more clearly one is able to see it.

On the more immediate level of our phenomenal experience, we understand a situation in terms of the antecedent forces that have made it what it is. We are able to act efficiently with material things, that is, we are able to control them, only when we have understood the complex of causal factors associated with them. A person trained and experienced in some given area, be it fishing, medicine, or marketing, has an instinctive grasp, as it were, of the causal elements present in that process. He is able to act within the situation efficiently and to his satisfaction. We learn of particular causes only by doing. In practical experience, causality is the form according to which we plan (anticipate) the consequences of our action.

"Scientific causation," on the other hand, is just the union of the human capacity to organize events in a predictive manner and the regularity of events themselves formulated in such a way that it applies to all events of the same kind, with greater or lesser accuracy, depending upon the kind of organization intrinsic to the events. In other words, the applicability of a causal statement to phenomenal events is dependent upon the degree to which these events lend themselves to the human capacity to discover organization within them. We can for all practical purposes be quite certain that a well-constructed match, under the proper conditions, will always ignite fire; to predict with certainty the behaviour of processes within the sub-atomic structure of the match, however, as Heisenberg has shown,[35] is another matter. Certainty is less easy to establish the deeper one penetrates into the study of natural phenomena.

Causality, then is a multi-leveled category. It is the matrix for the order of all manifested being; it is a presence within man in the form of a capacity to organize events in a predictive manner and thus to comprehend them; and it has an individualized expression for each person.[36]

I have tried to set forth briefly various categories of being. The categories of feeling, mind, and understanding which have been discussed are not, of course, exhaustive; they provide only one means of articulating (and indeed only in a partial way) some of the implications concerning our human status in being. The categories, we find, must be posited in three dimensions; as they are beyond specific content determination, as they are forms or features of consciousness, and as they assume different determinations in actual individual experience. By positing the categories in this way we are able to give recognition to the essential, the universal, and the individual aspects of experience and at the same time to see the potential unity of man in being and the actual diversity of his experience.

Man as a Diverted Being

Phenomenally, we possess the powers of love, order, and will. But love, order, and will in our selves as we *actually* are differ from their presence in the soul in that they are transformed according to the dictates, necessities, and exigencies of life into a new form; phenomenally we possess love, order, and will as *needs*.

Whereas the pure activity of love in the soul is without acquisitive desire, in man as a *diverted being*—as a being who has become something other than his essential nature—love is a need. In our phenomenal diverted nature, love is that which ceaselessly demands objects for possession: it is a need for self-gratification. As diverted beings we are incapable of unrequited giving; we offer love only in anticipation of a personal reward or satisfaction. We make of love something possessive and thereby restless, rather than realizing it as a state of spiritual being.

The fact and significance of this diversion of love into a need can be recognized perhaps most clearly by observing it in one of its extreme forms, namely, in "romanticism." The romantic is one for whom another is of value only according to his or her ability to fulfill a love need. Romantic love tends to abandon something when once it is attained or appears attainable. It is only the unattainable that is capable of satisfying the romantic's overwhelming love need. Love then becomes a state of yearning. The romantic lover becomes enraptured with an object of his own (idealized) fancy and becomes engaged in the ceaseless pursuit of it. Nothing is loved as it is, but only as it serves to fulfill the needs of an enlarged egotistic self. The dialectic of love in romanticism thus culminates in a protracted and concentrated narcissism; the romantic discovers that nothing, absolutely nothing other than his own precious self is worthy of love, and he then retires to the gloom, morbidity, and pain of his own tortured subjectivity.

Our natural human love and the love of the romantic differ only in

61

degree. He expresses more completely, and without other restraints, what occurs within ourselves. (And hence the sympathy and high value which society often bestows upon the romantic as one of the hero-types of the race.)

As diverted beings, then, we desire ourselves in another; and we call this love. We discriminate in our desire, in our love need, and thus affirm implicitly if not explicitly that only certain objects are worthy of our love. We come to feel, like the adolescent and the jealous suitor, that the object of our affection must repay us in kind with an undivided love. In short, in our experience as diverted beings, love is restless and ego-centered; as diverted beings, we miss the possible richness and fullness of spiritual love; we transform it into a need.

The same process of change takes place with respect to the spiritual force of order. This power of the soul becomes in the empirical self the need to impose organization on our experience and to read everything in the universe in rational (humanized) terms. As diverted beings we need to order the universe, and we fail to recognize the simple difference between the reality of a world order and the construction of an ordered world.

The spiritual power of order also becomes, in the empirical self, an instrument for adjustment and utility. As "biological creatures" we need to master our environment, to assert our supremacy over nature and other men. "Intelligence" is the tool which answers to this need. Order becomes the need to resolve *problems*; it becomes something "pragmatic."[1]

Rationalists insist that there can be no rational contradictions in our reasoning about the Divine because we cannot entertain rational contradictions in Nature. This anthropomorphism of reason suggests that the criterion of order within our unreformed human intellect is largely "aesthetic," and as such is not founded on a real principle of order intrinsic to being. The canons of consistency and non-contradiction that are basic to this "aesthetic of the reason" are products of our minds, and this, because they are needs of our minds.[2] The niceties of a logical proof that please the logician, the simplicity of a law or the elegance of an experiment which delights the scientist—all reflect this (aesthetic) need of our intelligence for an ordered, consistent, coherent, non-contradictory world.

The diversion of our spiritual power of order appears not only in our intellectual activities, but also in almost all aspects of our daily lives. We constantly restrict ourselves to habitual patterns of action and emotional response. Most of our lives are spent in routines. Indeed, the usual ordering of our lives is most often nothing more than a blind repetition of certain necessary actions. These repetitions have their origin no doubt in the positive function of enabling us to avoid doubts and hesitations: to live, that is, with a reasonable amount of efficiency. However, they tend to become mere external forms; like lifeless rituals, they become wholly automatic and habitual. Real order is creative; it is not artificial, it is spiritual.[3]

The ordering processes of our intellect are disvalued, then, insofar as they fail to reflect the true order of the soul and operate in opposition to it. Chaos, however, is no substitute for an order based on diversion. The disvaluing of our diverted ordering processes is not an invitation to disorder but to an authentic ordering which genuinely reflects the spiritual order of being. This can be accomplished not by an anti-intellect but by the re-formed intellect of man.[4]

Turning now to our human will we find that it expresses itself, in our ordinary unregenerate way of being, as the need to impose ourselves upon things and to protect ourselves from them. Ordinarily we act in direct opposition to the freedom and power of the divine will, the eternal volitional force of the soul.

It is necessary to distinguish several principles within our will as it functions apart from its spiritual source. These principles are treated "phenomenologically," that is, I am appealing to a *recognition* of them rather than to a marshalling of arguments or empirical evidence to justify them. The principles, in other words, are not intended to be hypotheses or explanatory concepts in psychology (or "pseudo-psychology" in this case); rather, they are the stuff of immediate recognition. It is not necessary here to do more than call attention to them with the purpose of understanding how we function in this our status as diverted beings.

We look upon the world as a field of possible change. We demand, in fact, that the world be amenable to our purposes, that it satisfy our desires, and we are driven to "improve" it so as to make it accord with those purposes and desires. This drive within our will may be called the "creative principle" of will. It is restless and compulsive. Constantly frustrated it nevertheless continues to demand its due satisfaction. It thus functions positively as a source of external reform and negatively as a source of internal pain. It gives us, in short, the impetus to change our environment, and it gives rise to discontent when we encounter the oppositions to change within the environment.

In direct antithesis to these promptings to reform, there lies within us a "destructive" principle. It is that aspect of our willing which calls for the annihilation of anything that stands in the way of our desires. In our diverted will we desire the elimination of whatever impedes or otherwise prevents us from realizing some selected goal. This destructive principle is aggressive; if left to itself, it would be a merciless "will to power."[5]

Between the creative and the destructive, the forces of amelioration and of annihilation, there exists a "limiting principle," which is itself comprised of several forces.

The "image force" is that within our will which prompts us to put forward various self-images which we feel compelled to fulfill. We can easily recognize that we have a need for status in the eyes of others, and that this need binds us to society and gives rise to our constraining our desires so as to permit us to participate in society. This image force thus contributes to a restriction of the creative and destructive principles and helps to bring about a regulated social self.

Closely related to this image force within the limiting principle of our will is the force of "fear." "Fear," as we recognize it in this context, is a pervasive presence in our will which limits volitional activity and hence all forms of empirical experience. It is not so much an "emotion" (a transitory feeling of terror or helplessness with its accompanying physical manifestations of trembling and shaking) as it is a force which turns back upon the creative and destructive principles so as to prevent them from having us engage in experience which might unduly threaten our ego. Unlike the emotion of fear, then, which always has a particular object as its occasion, whether the object be real or imaginary, the limiting force of fear in the will has no distinct object which need arouse it: it is a continuous presence, it is always there in the converted will, and it always limits experience. Fear is present because we feel the need to protect ourselves from the wills of others—and from our own selves. We are fearful of not having our own self-images accepted by others, of losing our selfhood or individuality. Fear begets fear. Fear is generated in the presence of fear. Fear exists where there are differences.[6]

Our will acts as a unity. Simultaneously it seeks creatively and destructively, and limits itself. It is primarily hedonistic. It seeks pleasure and self-satisfaction. Whereas the eternal will of our soul remains content with itself and becomes thereby the volitional energy of a free, unrestrained, joyous creativity, our human will in our living actuality as diverted beings is ceaselessly unsatisfied. It is restless and unstable. And when a man withdraws from the burdens of this will (and without yet attaining to his eternal will) he finds himself replete with lethargy and ennui, with that weariness which Schopenhauer admirably expressed when he wrote: "... as soon as want and suffering permit rest to a man, ennui is at once so near that he necessarily requires diversion .... We see that almost all men who are secure from want and care, now that at last they have thrown off all other burdens, become a burden to themselves ...."[7]

Love, order, and will in their true natures are spiritual forces. In man as a diverted being they are needs. But why does this diversion take place? The answer is relatively simple, though the actual process of this diversion is no doubt immensely complicated. Man becomes a diverted being because life, as he is born into it, demands it of him.[8] Human life is a grand network of needs. We need to master our physical environment and to adapt our intellects to it in order to survive; we need to impose restrictions upon ourselves and upon others in order to construct a regulated society, in order to fulfill our natural capacities, in order to avoid chaos; as a social, biological, intellectual creature a man must necessarily represent a striving individual living in a world with other individuals. Diversion is a natural consequent for man as a social, material, mental being.

Whenever one is aware of the *distance* that stands between one's actuality—one's state of restless being—and one's essentiality, one is aware of being "diverted."

Whenever one is aware that one's own being is simply in the way of true being, that one does not belong in a reality that admits the possibility of perfection, one is aware of being a "diverted being."

Whenever one feels the compelling, almost torturous demand for an inner self-transformation, for the overcoming of ego, the rooting out of self-centeredness, one understands this fact of diversion.

It is a significant fact that the higher religions, with unanimity, have held that man is in some way a degeneration of what he was originally. He is a "fallen creature." The rationale behind the myth is that of diversion. Diversion is not, however, something final. It tells us why we are "creaturely," but it does not impose finality upon this status. There is, rather, within the very awareness of being diverted an implicit suggestion that one has the power to resist it, that one has the power to transform one's distorted, diverted being into a joyous state of spiritual being.

Man's Construction of a
Habitual Reality

THE THEORY OF PERCEPTION

There is no limit to the number of ways by which we may explain the
world of our sense-mental experience. For all philosophical explanations of this world are valid according to the extent to which the experience selected by them is accounted for, and no philosophical
explanation will ever be completely valid because it can only be an
organizing perspective upon some aspects of experience, which aspects
are themselves subject to constant change. Being itself an integral part
of the sense-mental world, the mind can never hope to attain a complete or wholly satisfactory explanation of it. In the world of our ordinary sense-mentality we are dealing with what Plato rightly called
"opinion." It is only when this world is seen from a higher viewpoint,
in a spiritual context, that its fundamental meaning and significance
presents itself to us. Still it is the task of metaphysics not only to view
lower orders of experience from more comprehensive positions, but
also to seek an understanding of those lower orders within their own
terms. This task is given to metaphysics for the reason that the existence of spiritual orders of being imply that the lower orders of our
experience, when taken as final and conclusive, act as an obstruction
to the realization of true being and reality. The world that we experience in our ordinary sense-mentality is not the real world of spirit. It
remains for metaphysics to determine the nature of that sense-mental
world and the manner in which it is not the real world.

In doing this, metaphysics must be largely dependent upon psychology. The facts of psychology—where psychology is taken as the
study of the actual contents, functions, and processes of our sense-based
consciousness—must be the basis on which we draw our implications.
We must first come to grips with the fundamental "how" of the
perception-conception process, and to do this we must turn to psychology for instruction.

Psychology, however, is not a single homogeneous science; there are numerous schools of psychology which employ different methods, work from different assumptions, and concern themselves with different types of problems. It seems, though, that the school of Gestalt psychology, as supplemented by several insights in classical Vedāntic psychology,[1] offers us the best starting point for this inquiry. Gestalt psychology has succeeded in eliminating many errors of older schools and its general methods of approach have proven to be fruitful in many branches of the field.

The term "gestalt" is defined formally and ostensively by two of the leading members of the school as follows:

... There are wholes, the behaviour of which is not determined by that of their individual elements, but where the part-processes are themselves determined by the intrinsic nature of the whole. (Wertheimer)[2]

When spatial, visual, auditory and intellectual processes are such as to display properties other than could be derived from the parts in summation, they may be regarded as unities illustrating what we mean by the word "gestalten." (Köhler)[3]

Gestalt psychology, which is primarily a theory of organization, conceives of a whole or of a "form," then, as a structured unit which is greater than (that is, possesses qualities other than may be obtained through) the mere summation of its parts. Unlike the analytic, associationistic psychology of the nineteenth century, with its elementary sensations, images, and the like that are built up into mental mosaics, the gestaltist argues that a form, a whole, a configuration is a self-organized field; a change in its parts will not by itself affect the forces which account for its wholeness. A form, in other words, can be transposed; it will not suffer loss of identity because of changes in some or all of its parts (e.g., a musical melody).

According to gestalt theory, the parts or elements that comprise a whole do not "exist" prior to the whole, rather, they derive their distinguishing characteristics from the nature of the unit in which they participate. Köhler, for example, states that "units show properties belonging to them as contexts or systems.... The parts of such units or contexts exhibit dependent properties in the sense that, given the place of a part in the context, its dependent properties are determined by this position."[4]

Gestalt theory is then led to postulate an isomorphism between the structures of phenomena and the forms of our psychophysical makeup that are involved in the process of apprehending those structures. It asserts that there is a coordination between sense-patterning and physiological brain-processes so that a one-to-one correlation is set up between them.[5] And further, by an "extended isomorphism," gestalten are regarded by some interpreters of the school as having objective ontological status: they do not come into existence merely because of our human ways of organizing perceptions, rather, they are taken as fundamental constituents of the phenomenal world.[6] And hence, as Gardner Murphy notes, "the first task of the perceiver, then [according to the gestaltist account], is not to create, but to apprehend the order and meaning which is there objectively in the world."[7]

In its explanation of perception, gestalt theory minimizes the influence that the perceiver's past experience exerts upon the organization of wholes. The gestaltist maintains that objects appear originally as structured units. Perception is made up, not of a "bundle of elements," but of organized wholes from the very start. "Perceptual constancies are natively given, are experienced directly ...."[8] A whole, in other words, is not a compound built-up of separate and simple stimuli, but has its distinctive character from the dawn of perception. A very young child will thus perceive objects according to the gestalt laws of perception.

In sum, given a physical organization or whole (W) which is constituted by parts (P_1, P_2, P_3, etc.), if at a given space-time the parts are disposed in such a way that (W) is experienced by a perceiver as a recognizable whole, as a qualitative whole (Q-W), with a formed patterning of cerebral excitations taking place in the perceiver coincident with or corresponding to the internal structure of (W), then (W) is more than the sum of its parts: it is a gestalt.

Let us take the following lines: |‾‾ |＼| . Following the laws of gestalt organization, the lines "close" in our perception into the configuration E N . Now it is clear that before these lines are experienced as E N, as letters of the alphabet, we need assume that the perceiver knows the alphabet, that he has *learned* to recognize certain physical marks as symbols and not merely as bare perceptual organizations. And if these letters were to have a meaning to an observer over and above their being simply indifferent letters, if they were the initials of his name, or if they formed a word in a language with which he was familiar, his experience of them would undoubtedly be different from that of an observer for whom these "ifs" did not apply. The gestaltist's notion of "meaning" as a natural concomitant of organization is thus incomplete. "Meaning," it is true, cannot be found initially where organization is lacking; however, "significance," "familiarity," "value" clearly tend to be imposed upon as well as suggested by perceptual organization.[9]

And it is also clear, as this is articulated quite fully in Vedāntic psychology, that in perception (*pratyakṣa*), in the process of assimilating the form of an object, the mind (*manas*) or "internal organ" (*antaḥkāraṇa*) of the perceiver undergoes a modification (*vṛtti*) and takes upon itself something of the character of the object. We become, so to speak, what we perceive. The mind is not a mere passive receptacle which takes in objectively given gestalts, it is itself active from the start in perception and, like all agents, is affected by its action. It becomes habituated to, and dynamically familiar with, a world. Any single perception thus tends to influence all future perceptions.

Further, it is obvious that in any perceptual process a time element is present so that gestalts are perceived only as a "movement" of form: to describe a perceptual act one would have to approach it from the moment the form is grasped to the moment when one's energies of attention are exhausted.

Our brief criticism of gestalt theory has turned on its failure to take adequately into account certain basic features which seem to be present in all perceptual experience, namely: the effect of the perceiver's past experience upon his perception (in terms of his giving meaning to the gestalt), the dynamic mutually effecting interplay between the perceiver and his perception, and the temporal dimension present in perception.[10] Let us seek now to introduce these factors within the general gestaltist orientation.

In order to give some measure of precision to the terms which are employed, various terms and the meanings that are attached to them are listed; then by the use of diagrams the interrelations of these terms, as they may constitute a very general description of sense experience, are indicated.[11]

1. *instantaneous space-time (i. s-t):* Analytically and by various modes of measurement we may articulate temporal divisions and sequences in experience. The term "instantaneous space-time" denotes just such a division: it refers to a given specified time and place.

2. *durational space-time* (Δ *s-t*): This term denotes a space-time continuum in a given environment: a spatial-temporal contextual situation that is bounded by specifiable limits. It refers then to any specified "passage" of space-time.

3. *perceptual field:* The totality of events that exist at an (i. s-t) within the sense range of a perceiver. The term refers to the totality of objects and happenings that are capable of being experienced by an individual at a particular time and place.

4. *natural focuses of attention:* Those events within an environmental context ("perceptual field") which, by virtue of their nature, tend to become the center of a perceiver's attentive energies. Events such as the chiming of a clock, the sound of thunder, an abrupt movement, tend to demand one's attention by the force with which they occupy part of the "perceptual field." The "natural focuses of attention" tend to elicit responses from a perceiver by forcing their way, as it were, into his consciousness.

5. *perceived-event gestalt:* The perceptual form or whole which an individual selects or responds to from the "perceptual field" at any given (i. s-t). It is the pure gestalt: the perceived form as it is apart from any special meanings it may have for the perceiver. (It is that perception which would be given to consciousness when all the preconceptions, learned responses, and so forth of the perceiver—all "sedimentations," to use Husserl's term—are completely suspended.)

6. *conceived-event gesalt:* The "perceived-event gestalt" as it is actually experienced by a perceiver at a given (i. s-t).

7. *function of perceptual organization:* That functioning in the nervous system which organizes the sensory data presented to it into "perceived-event gestalts" or, to use other words, that internal process of organization which enables a perceiver to recognize an organized whole, a "perceived gestalt" in the "perceptual field." Perception is an act of cooperation, as it were, between "objects" and "perceiving subjects." Whatever the precise description of this functional process of organization might be (and it would be the task of a physiological psychologist to make it), some such process clearly needs to be acknowledged.

8. *past experience of individual at (i. s-t):* The totality of an individual's experience at all s-t's prior to a given s-t that are formative of his consciousness. The term refers to the entire past experience which a perceiver represents at the moment of his experience, including the

effects of past perceptual experience as these acts have subtly conditioned the perceiver. (This includes not only past experience which the
perceiver can consciously recall, but also the past experience that has
worked its way into the "unconscious," if it exists, and can, in any
event, be reached only through a strenuous analysis.)

9. *state of consciousness of individual at (i. s-t):* The state of consciousness of an individual at any given time and place seen in terms
of the degree of its "activity"; the degree to which consciousness is
awake to the possibilities of its perceptual environment. At each moment one exhibits in consciousness a somewhat different degree of
"awakenness," of alertness. The term denotes just that degree which
is present and operative at any specified time and place.

10. *emotional-intellectual-physical needs of individual at (i. s-t):*
The totality of the needs present in an individual at a given place and
time. Experience is always determined in part by the experiencer's
special needs.[12] The term refers to the state of being of an individual
at a given place and time as this can be expressed in terms of his various emotional, intellectual, and physical needs.

11. *emotional-intellectual-physical capacities of individual at (i. s-t):*
The totality of the capacities present in an individual at a given place
and time. At any given moment an individual represents a state of
being that can be described in terms of his capacities to attend to objects, to respond to problems, to endure strains, and so forth. The state
of an individual's operative capacities varies immensely from time to
time and is a result of many complex interrelated factors—everything
from the individual's physical health to the state of the weather.

12. *existent interest of individual at (i. s-t):* The special state of interest present in an individual at a given place and time. Interest is
clearly a result of needs and capacities. We sustain interest in something to the degree to which it fulfills our needs and to which we are
capable of responding to it. The term "existent interest" refers to the
actual interest, in kind and degree, that an individual represents at a
given place and time.

13. *activated disposition to attend of individual at (i. s-t):* The term
denotes the actual act of attending as it expresses an individual's
"existent interest." It is the active side of that interest; that is, it is the
"existent interest" of an individual as it is actuated in experience and
as it is itself partially determined by the objects of experience.

14. *memory-function A:* That functioning within consciousness which enables an individual to "conceptualize," to give meaning to a "perceived-event gestalt" at any given place and time. The term denotes the function of memory as it becomes in perceptual experience a tendency or disposition to impute a given meaning to a selected form.[13]

15. *activated disposition to conceptualize of individual at (i. s-t):* That functioning within consciousness which transforms the selected "perceived-event gestalt" into a "conceived-event gestalt." The term denotes the activated tendency of an individual to conceptualize a selected gestalt in his own special way. At every instant of consciousness an individual has an existing disposition to unite a pattern of meaning with, or impose a special significance on, the gestalt that he selects and receives. And it is here that the influence of language upon perception is most clearly manifest. The disposition to conceptualize is dependent to a great extent upon the individual's ability to relate the objects of his experience to a linguistic framework. For the most part whenever we experience an object that has a name or some other linguistic designation with which we are familiar, we unite the word to the object and experience the two as one. "Before the intellectual work of conceiving and understanding phenomena can set in," writes Ernst Cassirer, "the work of naming must have preceded it, and have reached a certain point of elaboration .... All theoretical cognition takes its departure from a world already pre-formed by language ...."[14] The term "activated disposition to conceptualize" refers to the entire structure of meaning that an individual brings to his experience. It is the active side of "memory-function *A*"; it is that which enables a perceiver to see the world of his phenomenal experience as something familiar, as something imbued with meaning. (See diagram 1, p. 74.)

16. *memory-function B:* That functioning within consciousness which makes possible the organization and integration over a space-time sequence (Δ s-t) of the selected perceived-event gestalts (which are *instantaneously* transformed into conceived-event gestalts) into a coherent, unified pattern of perception. Perception is an integral process: it is not in actuality split up into discrete, discontinuous gestalts. "Memory-function *B*" refers to that within consciousness which performs this work of integration; this work of imposing a continuous pattern of meaning over a given space-time sequence.[15]

DIAGRAM 1

*Selection of the "perceived-event gestalt" and its
transformation into a "conceived-event gestalt"*

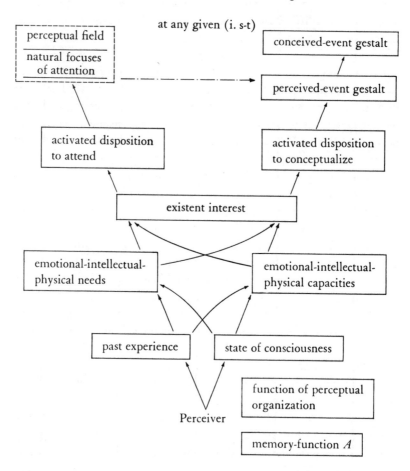

17. *activated disposition to integrate:* The actual disposition of an
individual to integrate and organize during a given (Δ s-t) the selected
gestalts into a coherent unified pattern of experience. It is the specific
activation of "memory-function B" over a given space-time sequence.

18. *durational gestalt:* The total series of gestalts over a given (Δ s-t)
experienced as an undivided whole or unity. Within any given spatial-
temporal context, with specifiable limits, perception is as a whole. This
term refers to that whole, to the integration of "conceived-event ge-

stalts" over a given space-time sequence. It is the resultant of perception. (See diagram 2.)

The construction of a "durational gestalt"

over any given (Δ s-t)

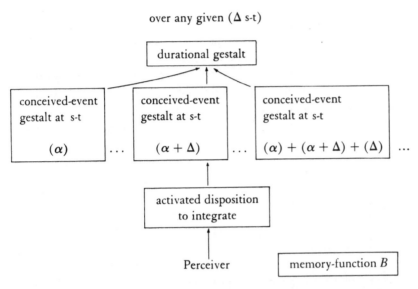

The process of perception has been broken down into some of its most basic and universal terms. It has been described first in static terms by freezing the process into a single moment and tracing the factors or leading characters which seem to make it what it is; and then in dynamic terms, in the terms in which perception actually occurs, as an integral mobility. Out of a totality of possible objects of attention (the "perceptual field"), at any given time and place, a perceiver selects and responds to organized forms and immediately brings his own history and present state of conscious being to bear upon them. His past experience, his present alertness, his current needs and capacities produce an "existent interest" which is activated so as to transform the bare "perceived-event gestalt" into a "conceived-event gestalt" and, over a period of attention, into the object (the "durational gestalt") as he actually perceives it. This process is, to be sure, largely unself-conscious. We habitually impose meaning upon the given structures of perception and consequently we see things in terms of that meaning.[16]

We see the world, it seems then, in such a way as to make thought and valuation possible—which is to say, we perceive the world in a highly limited and selective manner. If we perceived the world as it is in physical terms (as encompassing the full range of possible sights and sounds, e.g., electromagnetic waves), if the *Lebenswelt* were coincident with the "scientifically objective world," we would be lost in and exhausted by it. The invariants of our perception do not disclose the actual physical world. The persistence of objects as substantial individual things with the same qualities is the stuff of our perception, even though our scientific knowledge of things tells us something quite different. Our limited perception of the world thus seems to serve a definite biological end: our survival and our evolutionary development are dependent upon our *not* perceiving the world, with our present means of organization, in the way that science tells us the world is.

PERSPECTIVAL MONADISM

From our brief account of perception, it is clear that no two persons see the world in exactly the same way. Each brings to his perceptual experience a special combination of interests, needs, and capacities. Each molds the contents of experience into his own special viewpoint. Psychologically, then, each perceiver is "monad";[17] each perceiver views the world through a perspective. To an architect, a building is seen in terms of its proportions and forms, its textures and colors, as it shapes and creates a physical space and as it satisfies various human functions; to an engineer, the building is seen as a structure, and it represents distributions of weights, balances between stresses and strains; to the sociologist, the building is seen in terms of its capacity to house people, to satisfy the needs for shelter, for privacy and the like; to the workman, the building is seen in terms of his labor, his sweat and wages; to the owner, as it represents his planning and enterprise, his capital and perhaps profit. The architect, engineer, sociologist, workman, owner—each projects his own perspective into the object, passes over it, and sees his own interests. The truth of this fundamental principle of "perspectival monadism," that each person has his own special experience of the world and that he projects his "viewpoint" back into the objects of his perception, has won widespread acceptance. Greek, French, German, English, American thinkers, who tend to differ philosophically more often than they agree, all attest to this principle. For example:

I see everything I paint in this world, but everybody does not see alike. To the eyes of the miser a guinea is far more beautiful than the sun, and a bag worn with the use of money has more beautiful proportions than a vine filled with grapes. The tree which moves one to tears of joy is in the eyes of others only a green thing which stands in the way.... As a man is, so he sees. (William Blake)

Let four men make a trip to Europe. One will bring home only picturesque impressions.... To another all this will be non-existent; and distances and prices ... and other useful statistics will take their place. A third will give a rich account of the theatres, restaurants.... Each has selected, out of the mass of presented objects, those which suited his private interest and has made his experience thereby. (William James)

Man is the measure of all things .... (Protagoras)

Man lives and moves in what he sees, but he sees what he wants to see. Try different types of people in the midst of any landscape. A philosopher will only vaguely see phenomena; a geologist crystallized confused, ruined and pulverized epochs; a soldier, opportunities and obstacles; and for a peasant it will only represent acres, and perspiration and profits .... But all of them will have this in common, they will see nothing simply as a view. They will only get from their sensations, the shock necessary to carry them on to something quite different, to what they are familiar with. (Paul Valéry)

No man sees the world just as another sees it. (Goethe)

But how astonished we were to see that the grey sky had robbed the whole scene of its magic, and that the place we had thought so charming when we had walked in it as lovers was nothing but a dreary hotel garden. (André Gide)

Every organism is, so to speak, a monadic being. It has a world of its own because it has an experience of its own. (Ernst Cassirer)

And there is no limit to possible perspectives. For each individual represents not a static, single perspective, but a dynamic, ever-shifting series of them. As his experience is enlarged, his viewpoints undergo alteration, they grow in breadth and depth. The construction of a perspective is thus immensely complicated; every aspect of a man's being is reflected in it: his innate predispositions, his "unconscious repressions," his conscious selectivities, all enter into it. And no single

perspective embraces the whole of actuality. Each is necessarily confined to only a part of it. At any one time, one can attend to only a
very limited number of existents, one can direct one's interests only to
some one or more features of life's multiplicity. Also, perspectives overlap; they do not, for the most part, exclude each other. All perspectives
are at once individual and universal; they reflect particular experiences
and they address themselves to similar possibilities. Although no com-
pounding of perspectives can ever exhaust an object, they do complement one another and provide us with the possibility of a rich understanding of our sense-mental world.

It has been said that perspectives are at once individual and universal. The perceived-event gestalts are "objectively" given; the limits
of our sense organs are basically similar (variations between individuals in their capacity to discern wavelengths are negligible); natural
focuses of attention tend to be identical for most persons in a given
environment, and so on. In the language of ontology, each person
functions through similar categories of feeling, mind, and understanding, and each person meets these categories in their objective embodi-
ments. Each person is a world to himself, but he is not just a world to
himself. Experience is, as it were, socialized.[18] There are levels to
human experience, and all men participate in certain of them. Each
person is a world to himself and exists in a world common to all.
William James brings this out in an especially clear way when he
writes:

In my mind and your mind the rejected portions and the selected portions
of the original world stuff [the possible contents of perception] are to a
great extent the same. The human race as a whole largely agrees as to
what it shall notice and name, and what not. And among the noticed parts
we select in much the same way for accentuation and preference or sub-
ordination and dislike.[19]

He goes on to say, however:

There is . . . one entirely extraordinary case in which no two men ever are
known to choose alike. One great splitting of the whole universe into two
halves is made by each of us. . . . When I say that we all call the two halves
by the same name, and that those names are *"me"* and *"not-me"* respec-
tively, it will at once be seen what I mean. The altogether unique kind of
interest which each human mind feels in those parts of creation which it
can call *me* or *mine* may be a moral riddle, but it is a fundamental psychological fact. No mind can take the same interest in his neighbor's *me* as in

his own. The neighbor's *me* falls together with all the rest of things in one foreign mass, against which his own *me* stands out in startling relief.[20]

THE PLURALISTIC UNIVERSE

In our normal habitual form of I-consciousness, we view everything other than that which can be encompassed inwardly within that consciousness as something not-self: as something essentially other than, and hence alien and opposed to, our own egos. The distinction between "me" and "not-me" becomes the fundamental law of the ego. *Das Ich setzt sich selbst*, the me posits or affirms itself, according to Fichte. A "dualism," then, which is founded on the tenacity with which we cling to a separating ego-sense and to a limited surface self and mentality, becomes the law of our existence. We feel ourselves to be isolated in an environment indifferent to oneness and filled only with conflict and the painful struggle of beings instinctively and intelligently guided by the imperative of self-preservation.

A "dualism" founded on a rigid distinction between "me" and "not-me," however, inevitably leads to a pluralism, for that which is "not-me" constitutes a multiplicity. Through the natural psychological processes of perception, through "perspectival monadism," through the distinction between "me" and "not-me," we arrive then at a metaphysical pluralism. The objects, things, and persons which we meet in experience are taken as if they had a separate independent reality. We give different names to things, discern different forms within them, ascribe different characteristics and qualities to them, and regard them as separate, as distinct, as independent.

In our first physical condition as infants, we are only passively affected by the world of sense, and we identify ourselves entirely with it. We see everything, through dull perception, as one. An external world as such has no existence for us.[21] As we mature, however, and extend our field of action we become increasingly aware of differences, we begin to regard the world "objectively." We sever ourselves from it and look upon it as the field for our personal life adventure. The whole process of learning becomes one of recognizing differences, of understanding things with greater or lesser clarity, by contrasting things with each other and by classifying their characteristics. We learn the nature of the various kinds of things we encounter and refine our judgment, taste, and sensibility with respect to them. Finally, we begin to reason about the world and we do so according to a logic which is itself founded on the distinction between subject and object, knower and thing known.[22]

There is thus a natural genesis to the metaphysical position of pluralism. It is a natural stage in the growth of the mind from a primitive naturalistic monism to a spiritual non-dualism. It is a natural expression of man as a diverted being.

THE CONSTRUCTION OF VALUE HIERARCHIES

The last element to call attention to in our making of a "habitual reality" is that of valuation. It can easily be shown that we see the world always through distinctive processes of valuation—processes that develop out of our multitudinous relations with the world. The moment we attain to a certain degree of maturity we become appraisers. We see other persons in terms of their character or personality or intelligence, as these compare with our own; we see material things in terms of their utility and beauty, as they may benefit and delight us or injure and repulse us; laws, institutions, societies are regarded by their capacity to insure our rights and guarantee our liberties; in a word, "good" and "bad" and all that lies between them are everywhere imposed by us upon existence. Every act of our perception comes to involve a process of valuation. At every moment of consciousness we cease to take the simple pluralism of objects which we believe to constitute our world as one-dimensional, that is as equal—for we learn that when everything is equal it is meaningless. Graduation is the natural product of valuation. From value discriminations we construct value hierarchies and in turn impose these upon the world. Valuation is not only a conscious discriminating process, it is also an unconscious or habitual process: the moment we perceive, imagine anything, our value hierarchies clearly are brought into play.

An attempt has now been made to trace the elements which enter into our formation of a *habitual* reality. We have seen that through the exigencies of life we divert the forces which lie within our essential nature into needs; through the natural processes of our sense-mental functions, we impose various meanings, values, and distinctions on everything that we meet with in experience. *Habitual reality* is thus the imposition of ourselves, as diverted beings, upon Reality. Habitual reality, the world of our making within the subject/object framework of experience, is the veil which separates us from the One.

Human Teleology

I have pointed out earlier that there exists in man a basic psychological function, the function of *attending*. The presence of this function, as it is grounded in the complexities of our psychological makeup, leads to the fact that the life of man is dependent upon his doing something, upon his attending to some aspect, sphere, or domain of experience. Except for very limited periods, man is unable to do nothing and exist. Even the dullest intellect, the least developed sensibility, would, if placed in a position of non-activity, indulge in desire, itself an act. Anyone who could refrain from all action, thought, creativity, desire, and not pass into oblivion and unconsciousness, would have succeeded in transcending one of the most basic human conditions. He would in fact have achieved self-realization. So long then as a man is, in his actuality, partly conditioned by his physical and mental nature, the process of his life will be a movement away from, as well as toward, the fullness of his essential being.

The word "teleology" is derived from the Greek *telos*, meaning purpose or end. The idea of a teleological or purposive pattern in Nature as a whole has, in modern philosophy, been more or less discredited. Since Spinoza and Hume, Darwin and Nietzsche, the most common statement on teleology is that Nature may exhibit purposes but that when taken as a whole it is essentially purposeless; at least, that is to say, man is incapable of discerning within Nature a single guiding principle, final cause, or entelechy. Still philosophy holds to the certainty that man is a purposive creature, that the human being is guided in his activity by purposes, whether they are rational or irrational in nature.

What then is the structure, the generic traits, of our human purposive life-movement? What are the most basic principles or tendencies by and through which our individual human activity is informed? It seems that there exist in human nature, in man as a physical, emotional, mental being, several opposing tendencies which, when taken as "instinctive imperatives" of his ego, become the *motives* by and through which he seeks to direct his development. Man desires to *individualize*, to *universalize*, and to *dissolve* his phenomenal or ego-istic self.

To individualize oneself means to solve, in a special existential and social manner, the problem of personal identity. It means to know oneself in terms of one's self-image and one's actual self-fulfillment; it means to establish one's place in a social environment. Entering into multifarious relations with others, one discovers "what to do" and performs one's tasks so as to mold oneself according to the demands and necessities of the relations. Besides entering into these transforming relations with others, however, to individualize oneself requires that one separate oneself from others. One becomes an individual when one retains an untouched vitality within the sanctity of one's own being; one becomes an individual when one possesses inwardly various aspects of existence that are intimate to oneself alone.

Following this tendency, this motive, for individuation, a man seeks "to be himself," to act out the special quality of his needs and capacities, to exhibit a style of life, a naturalness and integrity, a behavioral consistency that is appropriate to himself; he desires that his name shall call up to himself and others an image of a unique personality, one with developed peculiarities of feeling, thought, and expression; he desires that his achievement in creating himself as an individual be recognized and approved. In following this tendency, then, a man seeks status in a social milieu. He needs to be recognized as a person and to have his place among his fellow men. Ultimately, then, the individual is incessantly dependent upon others. He needs the recognition of others in order to maintain his self-image as a unique being. He needs others in order to define his individuality. The existence of the individual, in short, is dependent upon his existing in the eyes of others.[1]

To universalize oneself means essentially to pursue the ability, through learning and education, to communicate with another on the level of his highest intellectual attainment. It is the tendency to construct a self within the composition of phenomenal selves that is pre-eminently capable of communication and understanding. The universal man is one who grasps, assimilates and transmutes what man collectively has won during the struggles and visions of centuries. As a solitary, the universal man would be a paradox and contradiction, for he requires history. The universal man is throughout social in his mental nature. He is the fulfillment, as it were, of the "gregarious instinct." He is also the fulfillment of man's intellectual nature. To universalize oneself means to make of intellect the center of one's being. The universal man wants to know about types as well as about particulars; he strives to comprehend the ideas and forces that have molded his culture and to develop himself according to the dictates of a universal ideal. Whereas the motive to individualize prompts a person to develop uniqueness and originality of self, the drive to universalize directs a person to develop "communality" of self. Whereas the individualizing tendency produces the "character," the universalizing brings forth the "type" which embodies an abstract ideal.

The third tendency or motive informing individual activity is the motive or impulse for self-obliteration. Due to the more complex nature of this tendency and the confusion brought about by Freud's positing a "death instinct" (later termed "thanatos") which, according to his analysis, stands in opposition to those instincts that are in the service of life (eros) and aims to return the organism to the equilibrium of inorganic matter ("to restore an earlier state of things"[2]), a more detailed examination of this tendency is necessary.

The tendency to dissolve or obliterate oneself is manifest in many and diverse ways: we willingly turn ourselves over to totalitarian states, we lose ourselves through identifying completely with a group (be it racial, professional, religious, social, political, economic), we incessantly seek to get rid of ourselves, to be outside of ourselves, we ceaselessly deceive ourselves by engaging in a thousandfold activities which signify nothing except that they offer the opportunity for us to lose ourselves, to free ourselves from subjectivity.

But how are we to account for the presence of this self-obliterating, self-escaping, self-surrendering tendency which is manifest in so many aspects of human life? How are we to grasp the deepest meaning in this incessant fleeing of man from himself? What is it that man is escaping from and what does he attain through this act?

Man, we have seen, is a diverted being. In his living actuality man diverts the spiritual forces of love, order, and will incarnate within him into needs. Due to the exigencies of life, a natural diversion takes place in human nature, and the emotional, rational, volitional man as we know him develops. Man's self-obliterating tendency can perhaps be understood simply in these terms, that man, whether consciously or unconsciously, whether knowingly or unknowingly, cannot endure his diversion from an essential simplicity to an ego-centric complexity; man cannot endure the diversion of his incarnate spirituality into ego-dominated needs.

Not possessing the knowledge of this condition or of the means for a rediversion or transformation of the self into a heightened spiritual state, we are compelled to annihilate our superficial self, to destroy our personal identity; we are forced to become wholly another in order to avoid the pain of an aching subjectivity which, in this its natural condition, demands that everything be brought into it in order to satisfy needs. Self-surrender, in its manifold "secular" varieties, is a disguised attempt to rid oneself of the demand for transformation which one's nature ceaselessly calls for. In existential language, self-obliteration is grounded in the awareness of an estrangement from essentiality; it is the awareness of being apart from one's authentic being.

The self-destructive tendency which competes with the individualizing and universalizing tendencies within the life of the ego is not, as we see it, so much an escape from a shadowy libido as it is an escape from the dim awareness that ego-consciousness cannot comprise one's nature. It is founded on the erroneous belief that a mere obliteration of the superficial self-complex will release one from the intolerable tensions of one's diverted and divided nature or that it will automatically give birth to a deeper spiritual life.

The formation of personality, the growth of ourselves as individuals who are compelled to action, may be characterized then in terms of several tendencies which, when taken together, may be said to comprise the natural teleology of our phenomenal human nature. As persons, we strive to individualize, to universalize, and to surrender ourselves, to escape from ourselves, to obliterate our personalities. The "will to power" and the "will to live," all the classic teleologies of behavior have their roots in this situation of man as a creature who must act in order to live, and who acts egotistically as a diverted being.

The three basic tendencies which comprise the fundamental motives for human action are, however, opposed to one another. As structuralized within our ego-consciousness they yield contradictory impulses. Although in practice they naturally overlap and may be present in a combined form, they cannot be present simultaneously in their full active form in any one person at the same time. Most of us maintain a dull equilibrium between them; most of us, that is, do not permit any one of these tendencies to dominate completely the development of our personalities. The exceptional men in history are those who for the most part have followed one or more of these tendencies to an extreme conclusion. And it is the exceptional men who tend to suffer most keenly. A fulfillment of one possibility of self to the exclusion of others seems always to bring forth pain and frustration, for the fulfillment of any one possibility turns out to be unsatisfying if not illusory. The "individual" man is too dependent upon the recognition of others, and consequently his attainment of uniqueness is precarious. The "universal" man finds himself to be a mere collection of the ideas and cultural attainments of others and, due to his intellectual superiority, tends to cut himself off from the lives of more ordinary human beings and to miss thereby a common human identification. The "self-obliterating" man becomes simply a living paradox to himself. He is forced to live and yet is driven to negate his life; he embraces any new cult, any new idea that enables him to identify himself with something that he takes to be greater than himself; he is turned round and round and never finds a stable center of his being.

Man as a diverted being cannot be a fulfilled being. By substituting appearance for Reality, he misses the truth of his being; by being compelled to action without having a reference to the ground of his being, he becomes a restless, unstable and suffering being.

PART III

Self supernatural to itself. The I transcending its own self-image, its own habitual consciousness; the functions of mind enlarged, transmuted into different modes of operation, become united with a pure silence. Is that the essence of supernal oneness?

Or are there levels of world within primordial reality? The one invisible: world of creation, world of love, order, and will. Another visible: the world of habitual happening where a conceptual content is inseparable added to the intricacies of every dynamic perception and act; the habitual world constructed through intellect, the senses, the imagination, through the delicate multifarious processes of memory, thought, and feeling. The world governed by the act of attending; the disseminated and fragmented human world selected fleetingly through interests, needs, desires, and capacities; the world communicated through phlegmatic symbols and exquisite logics; the world of nature and of protean man; the world of our existence, the world imposed upon the Absolute as being.

The other a transformed visibility where consciousness now infinite enters into a new and formless order, meeting the One as valuable-being. Truth, Beauty, Goodness shining here eternally radiant, quivering as pale white light within light, with our human being stilled in the reticent image of night transformed from a complexity into the unity of a spiritual simplicity.

Within this other level of being, the self discovers that beauty is the sole means for the transmission of mystery; that the idea of a God transcendent to man is speakable only through beauty, through that which is born out of the joy and love in this other region of inner-outer being.

The Absolute as Valuable-Being

The truth of the Absolute, the truth buried in the furthest reaches of our human consciousness become supernatural to itself, is the truth of pure and perfect silence.

Transcending the contradictions and dualities inherent in every habit of the mind, transcending its distinctions and discriminations, the self, purified and whole, acquires in an immediate knowing the silence of truth, the profound ignorance of the wise. This silence is and is something other than the illusion inherent in all speech; this silence is and is something other than the unutterability of Nature and material being; this silence is pure and sacred being. It is truth reflected onto the soul, illuminating its depth, transforming its ignorance into a magnificent clarity; it is truth entirely human, entirely divine. Unable to be an object of thought, this truth, this silence, can be attained only through love and intuition, through the unity of our essential being with the spirituality subsistent in transcendent being.

Truth is silence. Truth is the stillness of the soul made beautiful through purity and love.

And Beauty is Reality seen by the transformed mind and heart grown beautiful in the love of mystery.

And Goodness is a state of loving being.

All human value hierarchies are inauthentic in the light of spiritual experience. They are subratable, and they are subrated by the Absolute. The Absolute is not simply another value among others but is so purely itself, is so purely blessedness, that it annuls all relative values; that is to say, it condemns all other values to relativity. When the Absolute becomes the content of consciousness, all other values are lost, are abandoned, or otherwise disappear. All habitual patterns of judgment become mere appearance, without substantial reality.

The Absolute is thus a denial of finite values, and it is a bestower of real values. It is blessedness, incomparable, rendering all other values as nothing. But white contains the potential for color and the many-colored splendor of being abides in whiteness and is the whiteness. The supreme value shines everywhere in being. Truth, Beauty, Goodness; silence, radiance, love are present whenever there is authentic being, being in the spirit. The Absolute is pure value and is the source of all real value.

The value of the Absolute, then, is neither a rationally determined concept nor an object of undisciplined emotion; it is neither subjective, a mere personal feeling, nor objective, a hypostatized abstraction from sense-experience; it is rather a state of being. For man, the value of the Absolute is an experience. It is the content of the contemplative mind attentive to nothing but the Divine.

And still there is a beyond. The transcendent value status of the Absolute points to something beyond itself. Like all statuses of the Absolute, it points beyond to the Absolute in its own wholly ineffable being. The Absolute is pure oneness. The Absolute is the one reality, the eternal presence of which nothing can be predicated. All else is illusion compared to it; all else is illusion when viewed as distinct from it. The Absolute is the wondrous Nothing which contains everything; it is the One and All of which nothing can be stated, affirmed, or negated in finite language.

And it is the content of spiritual experience. The Absolute may be sought inwardly through detachment, self-discipline, and knowledge, as a supreme truth grounded in the depth of the human soul; it may be sought outwardly through intuition and identification as spirit immanent in the universe taken as a whole or as a unity; and, through complete self-transcendence, through self-integration and purity, it may be sought as value beyond existence, as an absolute transcendence. The Absolute is a unity; its different statuses represent different presentations of that unity and also different ways in which it is approached and experienced. The Absolute may be experienced in its status of creative being, as a unity of love, order, and will; it may be experienced in its status of being, as a unification of the diverse categories of being as they are in their pure eternality; it may be experienced in its status of valuable-being, as truth, beauty, and goodness. The Absolute as the content of spiritual experience is at once a creative abyss, the structure of being, and the supreme value—and it is "that" of which nothing can be predicated.

Man's Transcendental Self

It is not the ordinary mental, volitional, or emotional sides of human nature, taken singly or conjunctively, that enable man to attain to transcendent spiritual realization. Intellect, reason, our ordinary consciousness do not bring us into an intimate unity with the Divine. The human mind functions only in multiplicity; transcendence is an ineffable oneness; intellect and reason function only in the presence of forms, in time, with relations; transcendence is the unformed, the timeless, the comprehensive—it is the going beyond all such contrasts and dualities. It must then be a "transcendental self" within man that enables him to pursue successfully a transcendent spiritual quest, a realization of spiritual value.

The lower cannot explain the higher. The nature of the "transcendental self" cannot be explained adequately by our minds when they are functioning on this a lower level of consciousness. We can *describe* a "transcendental self" in terms of the inherently limited concepts available to us from psychology and philosophy by contrasting it with the more ordinary functions of consciousness and mental life, and we can see what it entails within these abstract terms; we cannot *explain* it, and we ought not to seek to explain it away.

THE PSYCHOLOGICAL DIMENSION OF THE
"TRANSCENDENTAL SELF"

Psychologically the "transcendental self" of man represents a state of consciousness without qualification. It is the state of a comprehensive, free, and joyful awareness in which the truth of oneness is obtained. "Transcendental consciousness," then, is not to be confounded with a "subconscious" or "unconscious" or with a state of being in which consciousness is annihilated. The "transcendental consciousness" is not directly related to a "subconscious," at least insofar as it cannot be reduced to the fears, tensions, and repressions which are held to be the stuff of that consciousness subliminal to our ordinary threshold. The major characteristics of "transcendental consciousness" are exactly the opposite of those of the "subconscious." When it is effected within us, we are free from fear, free from difference, free from all tension: we are at-one with a supreme spiritual unity. "Transcendental consciousness" is also radically different from a state of "no-consciousness," for whereas the latter, if it is possible, would lead only to a void, the former, which is possible, leads to and is itself an immeasurable richness and fullness of being. It brings us to the superconceptual value domain of the Absolute and to the purity of its ineffable transcendent being.

According to existential phenomenology, consciousness is intentional: consciousness means consciousness *of* something or other. Now this is certainly the case with our ordinary waking consciousness (as pointed out before, and as substantiated by various experiments that psychologists have carried out in sensory deprivation, our being awake and ordered requires a dynamic relationship between subject and object); but it is not the case with that state of consciousness associated with spiritual experience, for here consciousness is at-one with the all-comprehensive consciousness of the Divine.[1]

Our ordinary waking consciousness is never wholly fixed or stable; rather, it is engaged alternately in thinking, relaxing, dreaming, and so forth; it ceaselessly shifts to different objects and to different aspects of a single object; it constantly lapses into disinterest and is freshly stimulated by other interests. Further, our ordinary power of consciousness is bound to "partiality"; we never see things all at once, we never think in comprehensive totalities, rather, we see and think in terms of selected, and thereby limited, objects and ends.

Transcendental consciousness is the transcending of these characteristics, and it is something more than that. In transcendental consciousness, there is a timeless simultaneity, a complete and comprehensive vision, an awareness of the Whole.

But not all men, and indeed only a few men, have realized this in their own experience. Most of us possess only that consciousness which confines us to our habitual reality. Consciousness within man is partly manifest and partly hidden. Consciousness varies in different men according to their different stages of mental and spiritual growth. Consciousness is thus actualized in different men according to their ability to permit it access to their lives.

It follows then that an "evolution of consciousness," about which one hears so much these days, represents a choice by man. We are essentially free to choose the level of life on which we live—be it a wholly external life of action wherein we follow only our natural needs and desires, a life controlled by intelligence and reason, or a life of the spirit which at once completes and transcends the sensuous and mental planes and brings us into an intimate contact with the truths and values of the Absolute. An evolution of consciousness is a self-transcending process which leads to a realization of the potentialities of our nature.

Transcendental consciousness, the psychological aspect of the "transcendental self," is thus a power of awareness which arises from unmixed attention, from pure attentiveness to the Divine; it represents a purification and integration of the otherwise disparate functions of ordinary waking consciousness, it frees one from the boundaries of one's habitual reality.

THE EPISTEMOLOGICAL DIMENSION OF THE
"TRANSCENDENTAL SELF"

Through the functions of our ordinary mentality we see parts only of the manifestation of the Absolute and treat them as if they were separate and distinct. When the "transcendental self" is present in experience we see things through the whole, we apprehend truth through the overcoming of the distinction between knower and thing known.

This knowledge is fundamentally a knowledge of value: it is knowledge of Self, it is knowledge of the Absolute. In contrast to the more normal processes of thought, where always in a form of self-consciousness, utilizing categories, forms, and abstractions, we strive to establish relations between objects of appearance, between one idea and another, to understand their structures and appropriate their meanings, in contemplative knowing, in knowledge obtained by identity, we attain to an immediacy of direct comprehension. Thought moves in opposites and separates itself from the objects which are thought of: in knowledge by identity this separation no longer exists; the subject "knows" the Absolute through the Absolute; oneness and unity, but not "understanding," are obtained. Our intellectual understanding cannot grasp in its own terms the precise nature of its "object" or the content which is disclosed when the distinction between subject and object is overcome. It must rest content with an "unknowing knowing." Upon returning to our ordinary separative consciousness we discover always that a certain ignorance with respect to the contents of this noetic act necessarily results. Our mind is unable to grasp, in its true nature, the content of the overcoming of the subject/object situation.[2]

All spiritual knowledge culminates, then, as far as our ordinary understanding is concerned, in an "unknowing knowing." It also leads to a transformation of all one's prior knowledge. One of the most distinctive characteristics of the epistemic dimension of the "transcendental self" is the transformation of our ordinary knowledge in the light of new values. The "realm of fact" is perceived in the "realm of value" and is infused with the supreme values of the One. Ordinary knowledge, knowledge by division, observation, abstraction, loses its hold upon us and is seen in its proper place in the whole. All rational knowledge is transformed in the "transcendental self" when once the supreme values of that which unifies all knowledge in its pristine oneness has been beheld.[3]

Knowledge by identity, knowledge through our "transcendental self" thus makes possible and indeed necessary a *hierarchy* of knowledge. We are led on the basis of a knowledge from the viewpoint of the One to see the relative place of all other modes of knowing. Abstract knowledge, scientific knowledge, knowledge through sensuous intuition, all assume their place in the viewpoint of that knowledge by identity, in that Truth, in that Silence where all is contained.

For a metaphysics which attempts to organize the contents of spiritual experience and to exhibit their implications, a hierarchy of knowledge is a necessity, for it is necessary that we understand that what may be taken as true to one level of consciousness and being may be altogether inadequate and indeed illusory to another level of consciousness and being. All knowledge by distinction, in contrast to knowledge by identity, is only "relative" knowledge; that is to say, it possesses truth only relative to various limited levels of consciousness and being. The distinction between *I* and *you* is a truth for our consciousness as it functions in its habitual, separative modes; it is not a truth of essential being. Relative knowledge, relative truth, is that which originates from our habitual processes of thought and observation, as these are related to what is taken as an external world. And there are degrees of adequacy within it. Some ideas have greater relative truth than others—whether the criterion of truth be one of correspondence, coherence, or utility. A hierarchy of truth, then, contains an implicit "dualism" and a graduated scale within the lower form of that dualism.

Two implications of primary importance may be derived from this. First, it follows that all metaphysical doctrines, religious dogmas, social ideas and ideals have only a *provisional* truth value. They are applicable at best only to a limited sphere of being and, in strictly human terms, to only a limited sphere of historical experience. No doctrine, dogma, idea, or ideology is thus worthy of a *fanatical* commitment; for each is necessarily touched with illusion. One would commit what we may call "the fallacy of mis-placed finality" if one were to bestow ultimacy on any idea (or idea-ology). All ideas which are grounded in the separation of self from the Absolute lack finality precisely because of their relativity. Their partial truth or value lies in the relative adequacy with which they encompass mentally the complex field of human experience and guide the energies of life into a higher spiritual fulfillment.

The second implication of a hierarchy of knowledge or of truth is that thought can never "mirror" reality. There will always be a distance between thought and being because the processes of thought are bound to the "relative." The formed and the formless are incommensurable. The first implication tells us that the *content* of any idea has necessarily only a provisional truth value; the second implication tells us that the *form* of thought can never adequately reflect reality.[4]

Many attempts have been made in philosophy to bring thought into harmony with reality through the construction of systems of logic. By far the most influential of these is that of Greek logic as codified by Aristotle. It reigned without significant destructive criticism for over twenty centuries and is undoubtedly one of the most remarkable achievements of the human mind.[5] It has become so much a part of our ordinary thought processes that even today, except in moments of critical self-consciousness, we are its victims. The reason for its success is simple. It describes and articulates many of the actual inherent principles by which we ordinarily think. These principles or laws according to Aristotle are:

1. The law of identity: If anything is X, then it is X. (A true proposition is true.)

2. The law of contradiction: Nothing can be both X and not-X. (A proposition cannot be both true and false.)

3. The law of excluded middle: Anything must be either X or not-X. (Any proposition is either true or false.)

They are based on the assumption that all logical judgments can be considered as relations between classes and that the subject of prediction is always a concrete individual substance; its various attributes connote its essence and determine it. These laws, which are so much a part of our customary thought processes, are also based upon two other interrelated assumptions: that thought is essentially a quantitative process, and that it is dependent upon sense-experience as the source of its materials. For Aristotle, quantity possesses ontological priority. Thought is an object-oriented process which seeks knowledge of a thing's essence and its relations to other things. It is impossible to think without the presence of limiting forms. Thought is utterly annihilated in the absence of concrete substances, of quantities, of relations between objects. (Hence, the horror of the Greeks at the idea of the infinite; the infinite, in anything other than mathematical terms, meant the indeterminate, the irrational, in contrast to the sharply defined sense-world with its distinct objects.) Greek logic as systematized by Aristotle is based upon sense-mental (i.e., phenomenal) experience. Aristotle says as much in his well-known dictum that "nothing is in the understanding which was not first in the senses."[6] Aristotle's logic (or what he calls "analytic") constitutes in effect a characterization or definition of the phenomenal.

Any attempt to transfer this logic, this definition of multiplicity, to reality is fruitless. How many arid scholastic debates are the result of this transference? How many persistent errors of the mind are due to our inability to set aside the conditions to truth formulated by Aristotle in our attempts to harmonize our thought with reality? We say that reality is infinite, and we immediately conceive of it in sense-terms as a quantitative infinite, as a space without boundary. We say that reality is itself and is everything else at the same time, and we are buried in a contradiction. But reality is not known through phenomenal experience, and any logic with its accompanying habits of mind derived from phenomenal experience cannot be applied to reality.[7]

A second major attempt to harmonize thought with reality (but which was in effect merely another demand that reality be adjusted to thought) is to be found in the "absolute idealism" of German philosophy, as set forth principally by Hegel. Following the romantics, Hegel saw contradiction, instability, and discord everywhere. The function (and meaning) of thought was to exhibit the manner in which these contradictions are resolved and taken up into a larger rational whole. It was a significant, but by no means unique, discovery of German philosophy that thought is not a mere manipulation of abstractions from sense-experience, but that it is a dialectical *process* which moves from one given thing to another; a process which moves in opposites and which seeks to generate higher syntheses. Reality, according to Hegel, is an organic whole; every part of existence is internally related to every other part and finds its meaning in the Whole, in the Absolute Idea. The relation between thought (logic) and reality is set forth by Hegel in the most explicit terms. "The Real is the Rational," he asserts, and then displays in one of the most grandiose monuments of philosophical systematization how thought, if left to itself in an organic universe, actually unfolds itself.

For Hegel, then, *it takes time to think;* and thought and reality are such that any question addressed to reality requires a total exploration of reality in order to be answered. Truth is systematic coherence. A truth is that which is a necessary constituent of a coherent whole. Every element in the whole necessarily entails every other element; and ultimately truth is the whole alone, the one Idea, the one systematic unity.

Hegel's articulation of the philosophical thought process also attained a considerable measure of success, for it too describes how our ordinary self-conscious thought often works. Thought assumes the reality of time and becomes a successive representation. When addressing any one thing we are led inevitably to some other thing.

Reality, however, transcends sequential time and determinate spatial relations. The internal interrelatedness of things occurs not within an organic rational whole, but in the spiritual oneness of the Absolute. And the contradictions and contraries necessary to rational thought form no part of the infinite being of the Absolute. The Absolute cannot be made a principle of rational explanation. It is not arrived at as the final term of a rational analysis or argument. The "Absolute" of Hegel is an objectification of rational thought; it is not the Absolute which is a state of spiritual being. The logic applied to, and derived from, the "rational Absolute" of Hegelian idealism is thus manifestly inadequate to bring thought into harmony with reality.

Another major attempt to relate logic to reality takes place in "pragmatism." According to C. S. Pierce, its alleged founder, we are to consider "what effects, that might conceivably have practical bearing, we conceive the object of our conception to have. Then our conception of these effects is the whole of our conception of the object."[8] One ought to attend, in other words, only to the practical consequences of ideas. A proposition *becomes* true, as William James puts it, if it works satisfactorily.[9]

The implicit metaphysical assumption in pragmatism is that there is no reality to which thought must be in harmony other than that which is disclosed in the problems and situations of man in his practical (and scientific) life. The sole function of thought is to resolve problems. John Dewey, the apostle of the practical, expresses it thus: "... all logical forms (with their characteristic properties) arise within the operation of inquiry and are concerned with control of inquiry so that it may yield warranted assertions."[10] Thought, with its logical forms, is not a means to attain to universal truth; rather, it is, or ought to be, concerned solely with the resolution of "problematic situations."

The pragmatist's "logic" is also a part of our ordinary thought processes. We look to practical expediency as the standard and value by which we judge ideas; and we invariably transfer this working standard to the truths of reality. We want to know what meaning reality has for us in our lives, and we insist that its only value lies in that meaning. Whenever we conceive of reality as a means to some personal end of our own—be it happiness, immortality, peace—we are victims of the pragmatism within us. We assume that reality is responsible to us, rather than we to it.

Pragmatism thus resolves the problem of the relation between logic and reality in a perfectly straightforward way. It denies all reality other than the domain of "public experience." Dewey writes:

Scientific subject-matter and procedure grow out of the direct problems and methods of common sense, of practical uses and enjoyments, and react into the latter in a way that enormously refines, expands, and liberates the contents and the agencies at the disposal of common sense. The separation and opposition of scientific subject-matter to that of common sense, when it is taken to be final, generate those controversial problems of epistemology and metaphysics that still dog the course of philosophy. When scientific subject-matter is seen to bear genetic and functional relation to the subject matter of common sense, these problems disappear.[11]

But when once an awareness of the truth of reality is present in experience, the problem (which is indeed epistemological and metaphysical) of the relation between thought and reality cannot, upon subsequent reflection, disappear, for it becomes clear that the ordinary processes of thought are inadequate to aid our understanding of reality, and in fact when applied directly to reality result in some of the most drastic philosophical errors and theological simplicities put forward by man. These errors and distortions (which unfortunately have had practical consequences in guiding men's behavior) derive from an illegitimate transfer of the logics of relative truth to the truth obtained through knowledge by identity. They are founded on the inveterate demand that reality be adjusted to thought, rather than on the attempt to adjust thought to reality.[12]

Man's "transcendental self" is a state of being. It may be understood in its psychological and epistemological aspects as a state of consciousness whose native noetic power is knowledge by identity. Psychologically, the "transcendental self" is a state of consciousness whose distinctive characteristics are simultaneity and comprehensiveness. It is a purification and integration of the otherwise disparate functions of consciousness, and it is a concentration of the impersonal universal consciousness of the Divine. Epistemologically, the "transcendental self" is a noetic power in which the subject/object situation of ordinary knowing is overcome and in which a direct knowledge of value, an "unknowing knowing" and a "transformed knowledge," is obtained.

The action of our "transcendental self" makes necessary, in philosophical terms, the construction of a hierarchy of knowledge; and it calls forth a critique of the manner in which we erroneously transfer the logics generated out of phenomenal experience and our commitment to a realist-pluralist metaphysics to reality.

The "transcendental self" completes the ontological interrelation between man and reality. It makes a man a significant microcosm. Every degree of being is present potentially within him. Man's soul-life in its essential depth represents an identity with and concentration of the universal forces of love, order, and will—the Absolute as creative-being; his mental and sentient life, in its essential structure, a consanguinity with and manifestation of the basic categories of feeling, mind, and understanding—the Absolute as being; his transcendental self a unity with silence and truth—the Absolute as valuable-being. The "transcendental self" of man is man become his true being in spiritual experience. It is the completion of the essential harmony and unity which subsists between humanity and divinity.

Man's Relation to the Divine

THE EXISTENCE OF "MAN"

It was pointed out in a previous section, on the category of the "universal," that for thought a universal has ontological grounding only when the particulars that comprise it have a discernible relation to the essential. This is borne out by the fact that thinkers for whom the Absolute is but an abstract word most often have great difficulty in dealing with the concept of man in universal terms. For such thinkers individual men exist, but man does not exist. But man does exist, because the Absolute subsists. There is a species humanity, which is a living reality and not a mere abstract concept, because there is a higher reality to which the individuals who comprise that species may relate. With the subsistence of the Divine, each man mirrors humanity.

MAN'S ACTUAL-RELATION TO THE DIVINE

But no man can live in a perfect unity with the Divine until such time as he is enduringly at-one with that essential nature of his which is divine. Existentially, a man is driven to become something other than the eternal ground of his being. In his actuality, man is a *relational* being. With the presence of a separative ego and a divisive intellect a man lives in relation to, rather than at-one with, the Divine. He incessantly encounters distinctive "religious" situations. He acquires, due to his diverted status in existence, an "actual relation" to the Divine.

All denials of man as *religious* are futile. Naturalistic (or dialectical) materialism which looks upon the religious nature of man as an aberration is, in fact, but one attempt among many to resolve man's basic religious situation. It, however, is never able to grasp in other than the most superficial terms the nature of man's religious situation, for one cannot understand that which one denies or assumes to be merely the

101

possession of another. "Religion" cannot be treated as an object among other objects to be explained. This would elevate the explanatory capacity of the mind over and above all the profundities of the human subjectivity out of which these explanatory powers themselves arise and from which they can never be dissociated. Man as religious cannot be reduced to a thing capable of being explained by another man. Man participates in the unconditioned and hence remains partly, and in his depth completely, inviolable to explanation by the conditioned. Being religious, man ceases to be an object of explanation and becomes a being worthy of being understood.

The distinctive characteristic of man's "actual relation" to the Divine, it seems, is that of conflict. In his actual nature, man is a diverted being and a being in tension. For example:

The Truth is impersonal, and our greatest human interest is in biography. We are never something apart from our spiritual source, and we like nothing better than to appear as independent someones. We recognize in spiritual experience that the Divine and our own true self are impersonal; when we are apart from that experience we need to retain ourselves as personal beings. We are too weak to endure the truth; the truth that we are nothing, that we have no being of our own apart from the Divine.

We destroy the men who teach this doctrine and then worship them as personalities. We convert impersonal truth into a personality.

Where our limited selves are, the Divine is not. This we know, this we freely admit, and from this we are in anguish.

We possess an intellect and we are aware of the complete inadequacy of intellect to bring us into a direct experience of the Divine or to enable us to comprehend its nature. Still we are aware of intellect's efficacy in dealing with certain spheres of life and of the delight it offers us. Through intellect we are able to assert our superiority over physical nature and over other men; we are able to attain independence and self-sufficiency. We are fearful of abandoning our intellect for the mere possibility of a greater truth realization, for we know that with the abandoning of intellect we expose ourselves to demonic danger, to the "irrational," as well as to genuine spirituality, the "non-rational."

Who can easily say, "I am ignorant; I know nothing; I am immersed in ignorance"? Who can readily live the truth that the unre-formed intellect is a distortion of Truth?

The Divine is ultimately simple. We manufacture complexities in order to make our lives interesting. Where there is a complexity, the Divine, in its own pure being, is not.

The Divine is Silence. We have the compulsive need to express our-selves, to utter sounds, to make noise. Compared to the Divine, all sound is superfluous and is as nothing.

We come to a full knowledge of ourselves only in solitude. Yet we cannot endure aloneness. We convert it into loneliness and we are burdened by feelings of social responsibility. Loneliness cannot be brought into a religious relation, for loneliness, like all other personal needs, is rejected by the Divine.

We cannot bear to be that which we actually are when once we rec-ognize the nature of that actuality and learn what we essentially are. We become laden then with the notion of sin, and become engaged in the fierce self-encompassing struggle to overcome it.

The Divine is terrifying whenever the truth of the One is converted into a personal object wholly-other to man.

Our "actual relation" to the Divine is founded, then, upon the dis-tinction between ourselves as we actually are and the Divine or our true self as it essentially is, and it leads to a radical distinction between ourselves and the Divine. Religion, or man's "actual relation" to the Divine, culminates, then, in the question whether he is to retain an unregenerate I or become his true self: it culminates in his having to choose between diverted man and the Divine.

Angst is the pain of having to choose.

Contrite consciousness is the feeling of having chosen wrongly.

Estrangement is to take the false choice for the true, and to make of this falsehood a necessity.

MAN'S "IDEAL RELATION" TO THE DIVINE

"Actuality" is not the final term of human existence. "Religious situa-tions" do not exhaust the possibilities of spiritual life, for the Divine is not, as we see it, an empty abstraction or a trans-cosmic personal being. One can search for "ideality," for a realizable structure of ideal relationship between man and the fullness of being, between humanity and divinity.

Imitation

Man has the freedom to imitate anything that he recognizes as a possibility within himself. The essence of a religion possible to man is that of an imitation of the Divine.

The word "imitation" has here a meaning quite different from its ordinary application to natural things and processes. An imitation of the Divine is not a copying of an outward form, it is not mimicry; it is, rather, a forming of an inward likeness to the Divine and the reflecting of that likeness, as a natural consequent, in outward forms. Christianity once embodied this meaning in its idea of an *imitatio Christi*, but lost the profundity of its conception by confounding in practice the truth of inner essence with the form of outer action. Historically, the *imitatio Christi* degraded into the attempt to copy, by mortifications and suffering, the biography of Christ rather than the essential spirituality out of which his actions might have arisen. It attempted to copy the conditioned rather than to imitate the unconditioned.

Imitation is the quest for equality. It is a conditioning process wherein the conditioning agent is not physical nature, society, other men, or another man—taken in isolation—but the divine Spirit within which all conditioned things have their being. An imitation of the Divine is the conditioning of man by that which is unconditioned; it is the attaining to an equality of being with the unconditioned as manifest within him. It is the discovery of man's spiritual nature and the becoming of it incessantly.

Metaphysics becomes religion when a man matures from a knowledge of distinctions to an attempt to live, to grow into, to imitate and thereby become, the nature of the truth realized in his deepest intuitions. To imitate is to be. Man attains perfection of being when he has discovered within himself the absolute calm and silence of the Divine and supports it with a free inexhaustible activity.

"And so it is sad," writes St. John of the Cross, "to see many souls to whom God gives both aptitude and favor with which to make progress ... remaining in an elementary stage of communion with God, for want of will, or knowledge.... They arrive at their goal very much later, and with great labour, yet with less merit, because they have not conformed themselves to God, and allowed themselves to be brought freely into the pure and sure road of union."[1]

The ground of union is conformation. The ground of union is imitation. Man's "ideal relation" to the Divine consists in an imitation of the Divine.

Man's self-transforming power

Man's actual status in nature is that of a diverted being. In his living actuality man represents a diversion of the pure forms of love, order, and will within him into needs. Man, however, as his experience testifies, has the power for self-transformation. Man has the power to transform his actual, his diverted, being into a state of being in harmony with the truth of spirit.

To transform or to "convert" is different than to change. To change means to take the same thing and move it to a different place. To transform means to bring about an inner alteration which raises the individual to a higher grade of nature. Change is one-dimensional, transformation is multi-dimensional. In transformation there is an initial reversion of our nature to its original form. Here the presence of love-order-will is met with and known. In transformation there is the conversion of all the limiting and conflicting terms of our manhood into terms which enable us to attain to an ideal relation with the Divine.

There is no royal road to Spirit. Transformation is perhaps the most difficult task which man can impose upon himself. It is filled with the most bitter disappointments, the most trying demands; one makes progress and falls back from it to a point lower than from where one began; one conquers one aspect of one's diverted nature only to find another one taking its place; one is discouraged by others, even forcibly discouraged by demands made upon one by society; and there is no resting place along the way. Every time one stops, one is retreating; every time one thinks one has arrived, one discovers a chasm still to be bridged. But there is within us this power for self-transformation; man does possess the strength to conquer his distorted, diverted self. The power for self-transformation is not a magical or occult power; it is the power of the Divine urging us on to the completion of our destiny.

Purification
Purification is that process wherein everything inward becomes available or receptive to the infinite Divine. It is the becoming like-minded to the supreme values of the Divine.

Poverty
Poverty is a state of freedom. It is not outward destitution or self-mortification. It is rather the state of being without desire, without need to possess.

Detachment
Detachment is the act of attending, in quietude, to the divine Being. Detachment is attachment of the greatest intensity. It is attention totally disinterested, and thereby pre-eminently interested; it is attachment entirely dispassionate, and thereby devoted.

Prayer
To pray is to commune with silence. A state of prayer is a state of harmony between the soul and the undivided word. Prayer is silence; otherwise another part of oneself would be listening, and where the limited self is, the Divine is not.

Sacrifice
Sacrifice is the giving up of illusion for truth. The perfect sacrifice is the perfect self-giving to the truth: it is the free acceptance of all the conditions necessary to the attaining of Truth. Sacrifice is not a material offering, it is not a privation; it is that intensity of mind and heart that has no other object, no other attachment, no other purpose than the Divine.

Faith
Faith is knowledge, love, and power.

Faith is the knowledge that everything abides within the One. Faith is the knowledge that the human being is essentially at-one with the Divine. It is the knowledge that man may realize his divinity.

Faith is the love which reaches inward until it becomes love divine and extends outward encompassing everything in both unity and diversity. Faith is love, and love is joy and oneness.

Faith is the power to attain perfection. It is the power of silence working in the soul. Annihilating fear, it compels man to act, through love, in the knowledge that there are no essential distinctions. Faith is power, and power is peace.

And faith is the culmination of the relation that obtains between humanity and divinity.

Chapter Summaries

PART I

The Self and the Absolute

Self-knowledge involves a spiritual experience of a timeless, relation-less Self. This experience discloses an ultimate non-distinction between the Self and the Absolute. The Absolute is the divine reality, the silent oneness of being. It cannot be understood in ordinary conceptual terms, but it is nevertheless a possible content of human experience, a possible state of human being, and can be approached conceptually in symbolic terms.

The Absolute as Creative-Being

The task of philosophy which recognizes that there are no distinctions in Reality must be that of discerning the structures of being which are disclosed in many forms of experience. The criterion by which distinctions between orders of being can be made is "subration"—the axio-noetic process whereby we disvalue contents of consciousness because of their being contradicted by other experience. The content of non-dual spiritual experience cannot be subrated by any other experience and hence is Reality. In another form of spiritual experience, that in which the subject/object situation is harmonized but not transcended, the structure of love-order-will is discerned. Love-order-will is a level of being that is subratable by non-dual experience, but is not subratable by any phenomenal experience. It is thus taken as the creative ground of experience.

The relation that obtains between this divine creativity and that which follows from it is a relation not of "cause-and-effect" but of "conditioning." This relation is demanded by the Kantian criticism of rational cosmology and seems to describe best the experience in which creativity is present.

This creative ground of experience discloses an essential spiritual quality in all modes of being and it enables one to affirm the presence of love-order-will within oneself as constituting the human "soul." The "soul" may be known as manifest in oneself, but not as it is oneself. There cannot be a plurality of souls. There can only be the realization of love-order-will in one's own experience.

Ideals of Man: A Critique
There exists a close relationship between the kind of conception one has of oneself as a human being and the kind of human being one is. Historically the most formative Western views of human nature are the "natural," the "rational," and the "paradoxical." The "natural view"—in the form of scientific naturalism—seeks to account for the origin and nature of man in functional terms; but by confining itself to a surface pluralism it misses the depths of being and is unable to proffer a significant total view of man. Romantic naturalism, on the other hand, with its emphasis upon inner vitality and change, seeks to go beyond surface functions, but it likewise misses the non-historical dimension of being and consequently fails to grasp the true power of the will. The "rational view" upholds the sovereignty of human reason and looks to it as the source of man's perfectability. It is incapable, however, of grasping the irrational and non-rational aspects of experience, and tends to restrict experience within narrow bounds. The "paradoxical view" of man is expressed most fully in Existentialism and Christian theology. Existentialism has made important contributions to philosophical anthropology, but its emphasis upon the individual *qua* individual is a serious mistake. In the Christian view, man is essentially estranged from the Divine, but this rests upon a possible misinterpretation of Jesus' teachings about the nature of suffering, love, and the relation of man to the Divine.

A metaphysical-spiritual view of man, while recognizing other levels and aspects of his being, affirms the essential freedom, timelessness, and potential divinity of man.

PART II

The Absolute as Being
From the standpoint of intellectual understanding, the Absolute as creative-being gives rise to the Absolute as being; it gives rise to the

basic structures that constitute existence. These structures may be interpreted in terms of various categories. In order to account for the essential, the universal, and the individual aspects of experience it is necessary to conceive of categories in terms of three main levels: the subsistent, the existent, and the developmental. The categories of being are divided into categories of "feeling," of "mind," and of "understanding."

Categories of Being

The Absolute as being expresses itself in *feeling* as a flow of spiritual energy that is constituted categorically by "rhythm," "proportion," and "integrity." These categories are primary in the sense that they are necessary for the actuation of other categories and condition their efficacy. The categories of *mind*—"purpose," "memory," "the ideal," "equilibrium," and "continuity"—are generic features of consciousness and are necessary conditions for our ordinary integrated consciousness. The categories of *understanding*—"space-time," "relation," "universal," and "causality"—are principles of cognitive consciousness; they are terms in which consciousness is cognitive. Each category of feeling, mind, and understanding must be seen in its threefold status as a subsistent characteristic of being, as an existent form within human being, and as a developmental feature of all individual sense-mental experience.

Man as a Diverted Being

Phenomenally, man possesses love, order, and will, not as pure principles of his being, but as needs. Man "diverts" love, order, and will into ego-based needs. Love becomes a need for self-gratification and possession; order becomes a need to humanize all aspects of experience, and it gives rise to a "pragmatization" of intelligence and to a dull routinization of experience; will becomes a need to impose oneself upon others and upon things, and it becomes constituted of creative, destructive, and limiting tendencies. This diversion of man comes about through necessities of adaptation to physical and social environments, but it is not a final status of human being.

Man's Construction of a Habitual Reality

Metaphysics is given the task of understanding the nature of sense-mental experience in its own terms insofar as this experience acts as an obstruction to the realization of true being. As phenomenal, diverted beings we build up a familiar world of relations and concepts which constitute our "habitual reality." This "habitual reality" may be accounted for by the manner in which we impose meaning upon the contents of sense-experience, which is perhaps best described in terms of the concepts of gestalt psychology, and construct individual perspectives. A pluralistic universe arises through this process as well as fundamental distinctions between "me" and "not-me." Various value hierarchies become an inseparable part of phenomenal experience, and an individual "habitual reality" comes into being and intervenes between the self and Reality.

Human Teleology
Man, as a phenomenal being, is compelled to movement and action. And man is a purposive being in the development of his phenomenal nature. The basic tendencies or motives which govern this self-development can be seen in desires to "individualize," to "universalize," and to "dissolve" one's phenomenal or egotistic self. These tendencies do not act in unison with one another, and they make for the restlessness and instability of man as a phenomenal diverted being.

PART III

The Absolute as Valuable-Being
Spiritual experience discloses the presence of truth, beauty, goodness—the value status of the Absolute. This value status is a denial of finite or partial values and a bestower of real value. It is not a concept or an abstraction; it is a state of being. The Absolute is a pure ineffable oneness. It presents itself in human experience in different statuses: as creative-being, as being, and as valuable-being.

Man's Transcendental Self
The ordinary mental and volitional dimensions of our nature do not enable us to attain to transcendent spiritual realization. It is necessary, therefore, to describe a trancendental dimension of human nature. This can be described psychologically in terms of the various features which it exhibits, such as "simultaneity" and "comprehensiveness." All men possess this consciousness potentially, but not all men have realized it actually. Epistemologically, the "transcendental self" represents the

noetic power of knowledge by identity—knowledge of value and reality. This knowledge cannot be translated into intellectual understanding and hence culminates in an "unknowing knowing." It also brings about a transformation of ordinary rational-sense knowledge and makes necessary the positing of a "hierarchy of knowledge." It further implies that all doctrines and ideas have only a provisional truth-value and that the strict logical forms of thought can never adequately reflect reality.

Man's Relation to the Divine

In the depth of his being, man is not different from the Divine. Existentially, however, he separates himself from the Divine and becomes "religious"; he bears various "actual relations" to the Divine. The essence of these relations is one of conflict, and this culminates in his having to choose between his limited I and the Divine.

Man's "ideal relation" to the Divine, as this is grounded in the potentialities latent in the essential, is one of "imitation"—the forming of an inward likeness to the Divine. This attainment is possible only upon the transformation of the self from a "diverted being" to a free, self-determined loving being. It requires the attaining to a faith made up of knowledge, love, and power.

Notes

1. Goethe, *The Principles of Natural Science*, trans. F. M. Stawell and N. P. Wydenbruck (New York: Carlton House, n.d.), p. 96.
2. It has been suggested that this non-dualistic notion of the self is affirmed in both Western and Eastern traditions of spiritual experience. At first glance, though, it might seem that Buddhism (at least in its early form) is an exception. In Buddhagosha's commentary on a famous passage of Buddhist literature we read: "Just as the word 'chariot' is but a mode of expression for axle, wheels, chariot-body, pole, and other constituent members, placed in a certain relation to each other, we discover that in the absolute sense there is no chariot; and just as the word 'house' is but a mode of expression for wood and other constituents of a house, surrounding space in a certain relation, but in the absolute sense there is no house; ... in exactly the same way the words 'living entity' and 'Ego' are but a mode of expression for the presence of the five attachment groups, but when we come to examine the elements of being one by one, we discover that in the absolute sense there is no living entity there to form a basis for such figments as 'I am,' or 'I' ...." (*Visuddhimagga* [trans. Henry Clarke Warren], chap. 18)

    Buddhism distinguished five groups or structures (*pañca-skandhas*) of empirical selfhood. These are: (1) perception (*saṁjñā*)—the activities of the five senses and mind (*manas*); (2) feeling or sensation (*vedanā*) of pleasure and pain, etc.; (3) volitional dispositions or impressions (*saṁskāras*)—all the appetites, memories, ideas that are associated with past experience; (4) consciousness or intelligence (*vijñāna*); and (5) body or form (*rūpa*). According to Buddhist teaching, there is no substantial self or "I" which underlies or supports these structures. The individual person is constituted entirely of impermanent elements. A human life is only a succession of thoughts, desires, passions, memories, and the like, which are combined into special patterns of experience which endure in time. When the body perishes everything about the individual disappears except for a kind of psychic continuity associated with *karman.*

Anattāvāda (Pali), the theory of the non-reality of the *ātman,* or substantial self, needs to be understood, however, in both its historical and psychological dimensions. Historically, it is not clear just what doctrine of a substantial self early Buddhism was seeking to counteract. It is quite probable that it is not directed against the Brahmanic teachings in their original Upaniṣadic form, for it is easy to show that there is nothing in the Buddhist analysis of the self which is really incompatible with the Upaniṣads (in their non-dualistic, *a-dvaita,* dimension). The assertion that the empirical self is an ever-changing, unstable pattern of feeling, thought, etc. does not contradict the Upaniṣadic view; it represents only a different emphasis. In any event, one has to see just what function psychologically the analysis of the self is intended to perform. The goal of Buddhist thought is the attainment of *nirvāṇa*—the liberation that follows from "desirelessness" and "concentration" (*samādhi*). The denial of a substantial "ego," or "I," is clearly intended to function so as to shatter any pretensions to ultimate value that an individual *qua* individual might otherwise possess and thereby to destroy any attachment to it. In the *Saṃyutta-nikāya* (III. 66) the question is raised: "Is it fitting to consider what is impermanent, painful, and subject to change as, 'This is mine, this am I, this is my soul'?" And the answer that is given is: "Thus perceiving ... the learned noble disciple feels loathing for the body [*rūpa*], for feeling[*vedanā*], for perception [*saṃjñā*], for the aggregates [*saṃskāras*], for consciousness [*vijñāna*]. Feeling disgust he becomes free from passion, through freedom from passion he is emancipated . . . ."

3. Many statements have been made here of an apparently dogmatic character. I am not concerned though with constructing a "theosophy" or a "rational metaphysics." The former assumes that the contents of spiritual experience can be made comprehensible in detailed natural terms, and consequently it denies the fundamental religious import and richness of Reality. The latter assumes that supra-rational knowledge is possible to a mere imaginative reason and is entirely "precritical" in its constructions and vagaries. A profound skepticism of the claims of reason and of rational comprehension most often accompany spiritual experience. At the same time, however, the claims of the intuitive capacity of man are upheld, and although the special type of knowing which accompanies it cannot be translated adequately into lucid intellectual terms, the content of that knowledge may be com-

municated, at least practically, through conceptual symbols. One must read the symbols precisely as symbols—as pointing to a reality which is affirmed. Statements which appear to be dogmatic are, by intention, *affirmative*. They seek to point to certain fundamental realities that may be recognized.

THE ABSOLUTE AS CREATIVE-BEING

1. I have articulated this criterion elsewhere in the context of the classical Indian system of Advaita Vedānta. See my *Advaita Vedānta: A Philosophical Reconstruction* (Honolulu: East-West Center Press, 1969), chap. 2.

2. This would be a case which might nicely come under Husserl's description: "[Judgments and cognitions about the world] clash and contradict one another. They do not agree with one another, they are falsified by *assured* cognition, and their claim to be cognition is discredited.... Or the contradictions disturb our expectation of connections based on past experience: empirical evidence conflicts with empirical evidence...." (*Die Idee der Phänomenologie* [Husserliana II], ed. Walter Biemel, [The Hague: Martinus Nijhoff, 1958], trans. George Nakhnikian and William P. Alston)

3. A simple valuation or judgment of the sort "X is good" involves, to be sure, certain epistemic features. It presupposes some knowledge of what is evaluated and some kind of cognitive comparison between the evaluated object and other things. It does not, however, involve an explicit rejection of an object initially evaluated and the replacement of it by something else. Subration does involve these special noetic qualities; specific reasons are carried along as part and parcel of the rejecting-replacing process. They are brought forth by the very experience or insight which, because of its richer content, condemns the initial object-as-judged to the realm of the rejected.

4. According to Freud, however, whose attitude is here typical of many modern (reductive) explanatory attitudes, oneness in love is explainable as a kind of regression to infantile narcissism. It is nothing but an expression of the libido. (See his *Civilization and Its Discontents* and *The Future of an Illusion*.) The rather crude mechanistic materialism upon which explanations of this type are based have, for the most part, been dismissed in analytic psychology. But even if it were meaningful to say that all emotions derive from, or are forms of, a ubiquitous libido, it still remains true that *spiritual love is not itself an emotion, though emotion may well accompany its realization*. Freud, nevertheless, has rendered a significant service to metaphysics in that

he makes it necessary for one to distinguish carefully between genuine spiritual love and the more exaggerated emotionalism and eroticism which often seek to pass under its name. The test of spiritual love is oneness and transformation, the liberation from self-involved emotional states, the experience of union, of freedom.

5. *Viṣṭabhyā 'ham idaṁ kṛtsnam/*
   ekāṁśena sthito jagat
   (*Bhagavadgītā* X. 42)

6. Modern rational or empirical systems of metaphysics, it seems, have not succeeded in grasping adequately this order principle which underlies being. A. N. Whitehead, for example, writes: " 'Order' is a mere generic term: there can only be some definite specific 'order,' not merely 'order in the vague' " (*Process and Reality* [New York: Macmillan Co., 1929], p. 128). The order principle which is disclosed in certain types of spiritual experience to underlie being and to be pervasive throughout it, however, is most certainly not some "definite specific order" knowable by our reason or experienceable through our senses. The order principle of the Absolute is not a principle of explanation. It is a spiritual principle and hence resists confinement within any conceptual form. Nothing derived from sense-experience can form principles which are perfectly applicable to the spiritual structure of being. For instance, Samuel Alexander states that "order is a category of things because of betweeness of position in Space-Time" (*Space, Time and Deity*, 2 vols. [New York: Humanities Press, 1950], 1:262). The terms used to describe this very simple type and idea of order are obviously unsuitable for a principle of spiritual order. In Spirit there is no presentation of things in fixed, isolated positions. And order, like love, is not on the other hand something "in the vague." It is a power of that divine reality experienceable by man.

7. We are aware of possessing a volitional energy through which we direct our actions and by which we react to the objects and forces that confront us. We are aware that a large part of our pain, frustration, and anguish is the result of this energy, and, at special times, we are aware of being subject to the dictates of a volitional force which seems to lie deeply within us and to be less capable of control than our more ordinary desiring.

It is perhaps from these primary acts of awareness that there arise the multitudinous problems of the will, the solutions to which constitute so large a part of the history of philosophical and religious thought. The Judaeo-Christian tradition maintains that in spite of Providence our will is free; for otherwise moral responsibility would be impossible. Buddhism, on the other hand, which is here quite typical of Indian thought in general, views the will not so much as a locus of potential good or evil, but as it is itself the primordial cause of suffering (*duḥkha*). It recommends that only upon the extirpation of desire, which is the essence of willing, is it possible to attain to fullness of being, to a liberated peace, to *nirvāṇa*. Much of modern philosophy and psychology calls itself "voluntaristic." It asserts that the combination of instincts and desires which are involved in the will determines to a great extent all our mental, social, and psychic behavior. The traditional philosophical claim that the intellect may be a complete ruler and judge of lower impulses must, according to this view, be discarded in favor of the power of the "irrational." Nietzsche's "will to power," Schopenhaeur's will as the *Ding an sich* which manifests itself in diverse grades of being, James' "will to believe," are all so many different formulations of this attitude. However, whether we posit the freedom or determinancy of the will, the need to annihilate it or to exaggerate it, so long as we fail to experience its depth, our ignorance of its nature remains greater than our theoretical knowledge about or imperatives concerning it. It is when we move to a deeper level of thought and being that the real nature of our will presents itself to our consciousness as a living actuality.

But, one may object, philosophy as well as theology has often posited an "eternal will." There is, for example, the Stoic will which governs the rational order of Nature; there is Fichte's supersensible will "which in itself is law, determined by no fancy or caprice . . . but eternal, unchangeable, in which we may securely and infallibly rely . . ." (see *Die Bestimmung des Menschen*); there is the Kantian "free elective will" to which alone one can ascribe goodness. All are eternal wills, whether purposive or blind, moral or non-moral; but are they something more than concepts? Experience has indeed pointed to them, and thought has demanded their existence in order to explain what would otherwise be inexplicable (viz., morality). One is doubtful of their experiential value, however, simply because of the manner in which they have been put forward—as rational necessities. The "eternal will," as I must use the term, is purely symbolic and descriptive. It is a name given to a content of human experience. No other claims to knowledge about it can be made. The task of metaphysics in this context, then, is that of seeking to understand the implications of this content for human experience in general. It will raise questions such as: What does this content of experience tell us about the nature and potentialities of our ordinary human willing? Why is this content not a permanent possession of our consciousness?

8. When I say "must" here and elsewhere in this section I do not mean it in any traditional sense of rational necessity—e.g., a simple deduction from previously established or "self-evident" principles or an

elaborate demonstration that any other view or position would be self-contradictory or a Hegelian-like causal production of ideas—rather, I intend a somewhat looser but, hopefully, more meaningful kind of obligement, the fulfillment of which would provide intellectual satisfaction. Given the reality of the Absolute, the fact of the oneness of being as a content of human experience that transcends all logical or rational determination, no logic or system of thought has an ultimate ontological ground and hence all philosophy, all systems and theories, lack any ontological necessity, i.e., reality does not provide them with any necessary warrant. But with the presence of the Absolute, other forms of experience pose problems of their relation to the Absolute and to each other that can be resolved satisfactorily only in certain ways. The ground of this satisfaction is no doubt partly aesthetic (Is the resolution "simple"?) and partly rational (Is it "consistent"?). Once these and similar formal requirements are met (which are more a matter of what one cannot do, e.g., be inconsistent, than of what one should do), a metaphysics, I believe, when successful, exhibits the kind of internal necessity that we associate with works of art—a rightness, a seeming inevitability in the manner in which the contents of experience which it discerns are brought into relation with one another. The artist has his own individual notion of what is right in the relations between the elements he constructs and in the choice of elements he makes, and yet when once certain elements are present other elements and relations seen to him necessarily to follow—and so with the philosopher. And just as a work of art could quite conceivably be other than it is, so could a metaphysics. There is, it seems, something a little arbitrary in any interesting form of necessity.

But still necessity for philosophy is not entirely arbitrary nor is it exactly the same as the internal necessity of art. A metaphysics is like a work of art, but it is not itself (in any very strict sense of the term) a work of art. Once the subject/object situation is engendered, the "object" side of the situation naturally imposes certain requirements of its own (as with science). We are satisfied intellectually only when these requirements are also taken into account. We demand, in short, that a metaphysics be an *accurate* map of our human being and experience.

9. *Ṛg Veda* (trans. A. A. Macdonell) X. 129.

In the later Upaniṣads numerous descriptions of creation are proffered, many of which are not so much speculations as to the nature of a first cause as they are symbolic or allegorical statements about the contents of spiritual experience. For example, in the *Bṛhad-āraṇyaka Upaniṣad* (I. 4) it is held that in the beginning there was only the

Self, who in his complete aloneness became afraid. Realizing, however, that there is fear only in difference, in multiplicity, he conquers and dispels it. Still he is aware of his aloneness and desires a second. He then divides himself into man and woman, and from this division the human race, the gods, and the entire differentiated universe of names and forms (*nāma-rūpa*) is produced. Spiritual experience of at least one type which is articulated in the Upaniṣads consists in the reversing of this process. It consists in annulling all multiplicity, in transcending the sexes and the gods, in overcoming desire and fear, and in returning to oneness.

10. *Critique of Pure Reason*, trans. Norman Kemp Smith, 2d ed. (New York: Humanities Press, 1950), p. 394.

11. Kant's contention that the unconditioned is never a fact of experience, but rather always transcends experience (that man has no capacity for an intellectual *Anschauung* which goes beyond the categories of understanding and sense contents) was of course denied by the later romantic idealists such as Schelling. Schelling, however, gives many descriptions of creation (e.g., in *Die Weltalter*) which to Kant (as well as to all of us who are certain that a detailed naturalistic or causal account of a spiritual process is not one that is derived from spiritual experience) would be nothing but fantastic.

12. *De civitate Dei* bk. XI.

13. These same presuppositions are also present in the more scientific-orientated cosmologies of recent times (e.g., in the "emergent evolutionism" of Alexander, in the "creative evolution" of Bergson, and in the "philosophy of organism" of Whitehead). These evolutionary systems translate the idea of a biological evolution into a theory of cosmic change; the universe is viewed as a historical process in which complex entities continuously arise from less complex antecedents. But still the ground of this evolution is taken as an independent substantial reality, and the evolutionary process itself is essentially a causal one.

14. In a later section the category of "causality" will be taken up and analyzed in terms of its status and role in our sense-mental experience. I will not, in that context, deny the efficacy of this category; on the contrary I will affirm it. My purpose at the moment, however, is to question the possibility of a cause-effect relation being established between diverse orders or levels of being. My position is that one cannot reason causally across different levels of being; that one cannot employ the categories used to establish relations within the empirical order also to establish relations between spiritual orders or between a spiritual order and an empirical one.

The Absolute and the world, from the standpoint of reason, are different in kind; qualitatively they are incommensurable. In order to set forth a causal relation between two things, a minimum requirement is that they be of the same order of being. One cannot reason properly from an "effect" back to a "cause" when the effect is formed and the cause is formless, when the effect is substantial and the cause is insubstantial. Kant is thus basically correct when asserting that the causal category is rooted in the makeup of our intellect, insofar as we are constrained to use this category whenever we determine events by antecedent ones, but that it cannot be employed outside the limits of a sense-based phenomenal experience.

15. The idea of creativity which I am seeking to establish here has certain affinities with Spinoza's notion of "God's causality." For Spinoza (*Ethics*, pt. I, props. xvi–xviii), God or "Substance" acts "freely" from the necessity and law of Its own nature, and becomes the "immanent cause" (God, as *natura naturans*—"the cause of things which are in Himself") that we are translating into the vocabulary of "conditioning." The relations which follow from the dynamics of love-order-will are not in essence separate from their source, rather they partake of it. The relation between the conditioning power and that which is conditioned is an "immanent" and not a "transitive" one. The idea of conditioning, as I am employing it however, does not involve Spinoza's questions of "rational necessity," "efficient cause," and the like, simply because conditioning is looked upon as a spiritual and not a logical process. Similarly, the question so often put to Theism with its "transitive" notion of God's causality—Why, if a good almighty God made the world, is there suffering, pain, evil, and injustice?—is not considered. The ontological assumptions of Theism are replaced by others, and the problems of the former cease to be the concerns of the latter.

16. All attempts to reduce spiritual energy to a concept of physical energy (which science may use to explain natural phenomena) or to understand one in terms of the other, are futile. Spiritual energy and physical energy do not occupy the same level of being. Spiritual energy, the dynamic power of the Absolute, is not susceptible to analysis, it cannot be tested in a physical experiment. The Absolute, in this its status of creative spirit, is a power; a spiritual power, not a physical power. Now, in all ages there have been men who would put this spiritual power to their own purposes. They would seek affinities, sympathies, correspondences between this power and various physical events. In other words, in all ages there have been *magicians*. Not infrequently, when pursuing a spiritual quest, certain extraordinary psychic powers are vouchsafed the seeker. Energy is stored up in such a way that one's

ordinary psychophysical powers may be enormously extended. Attempts to control things in nature and in other minds through this energy, this magnified purified natural energy, have to some extent apparently been successful. Our natural science is not yet able to accept these phenomena as "real," as it is not yet able (and has not really even made the attempt) to explain them. The real aspirant of a spiritual life, however, *avoids* them; for they only immerse him deeper in the finite, in the unreal. *There can be no magic with respect to the Absolute.* "Spiritualism," "occultism," and all such "isms" have nothing to do with the real spirituality of the Absolute, for its power is purely and entirely in the domain of value. Plotinus, who was perhaps more misunderstood than understood by those who took over his teachings, writes: "Alone in immunity from magic is he who, though drawn by the alien parts of his total being, withholds his assent to their standards of worth, recognizing the good only where his authentic self sees and knows it, neither drawn nor pursuing, but tranquilly possessing and so never charmed away" (*Enneads* [trans. Stephen MacKenna] IV. 4. 44).

17. The story, of course, does not end with Kant. In German philosophy alone, subsequent to Kant, we have Fichte, Schelling, and Schleiermacher putting forth, on ethical, metaphysical, and religious grounds, a kind of soul-substance theory; but these and similar attempts found elsewhere, are generally put aside in the later part of the nineteenth century when materialism and naturalism, as grounded in biological evolutionary theory, tend to dominate. And in the twentieth century a rejection of the whole concept of the soul in philosophy (and most notably in the various behavioristic schools of psychology) is more or less taken for granted. This is clearly reflected in ordinary language where the term "soul" has come to mean simply one's general character or person.

18. The affirmation of the soul as a confluence of spiritual forces does not enable us then to solve the many traditional problems of the soul, e.g., the problem of the relationship between "soul" and "body." This problem is unanswerable on the plane of discursive thought, as "body" and "soul" do not occupy the same level of being; they do not possess the same reality. The soul is not spatially or temporally contained in the body; it transcends all categories of time and space.

IDEALS OF MAN: A CRITIQUE

1. For example, the so-called tragic view of man can be understood as it combines various aspects of the "natural" and "paradoxical"

views. It shares with the "paradoxical view" its pessimism concerning the perfectibility of human nature, and it draws from the "natural view" its ontological assumptions about the status (the independent substantiality) of the natural world.

In presenting these views I make no attempt at thoroughness. I have selected only what appears to be a number of the more significant ideas and use them for the most part as contrasts to the spiritual view of man which I seek to understand. Further, by bringing several philosophers together under one label I do not intend to imply that their views of human nature are in all points the same; rather, I am trying to indicate certain "core ideas" which these various philosophers have in common. Aristotle, Descartes, Hegel, for example, tend to differ far more than they agree; they do agree, however, in assigning to human reason a central and dominant role in human nature.

2. The "natural view" of man divides itself into two main forms: these are "scientific naturalism" and "romantic naturalism." Both forms give emphasis to man as a natural being who functions in a natural world but, and this accounts for their separation, each interprets the naturality of man and the world in different terms.

It is also possible to analyze "romanticism" into several kinds or types. For my purpose here it is necessary to call attention only to the distinction between "romantic naturalism" (e.g., Nietzsche and poets such as Novalis) and "romantic idealism" (e.g., Schelling). The difference between these two kinds of romanticism is especially apparent in their respective interpretations of the status of human reason or intellect. The romantic idealists were a new species of "rationalists"; they were concerned more with the logical development of ideas and notions than with the actual biological or temporal development of man. The idealists did not, like the naturalists, construct nor indeed encounter the paradox of man's seeking to transcend nature through strictly finite powers of will. Both kinds of romanticism, however, ascribe to the individual ego (whether defined as intellect or will) a central, and exaggerated, place in an organic whole.

3. Henri Bergson, "Introduction to Metaphysics," in *The Creative Mind*, trans. Mabelle L. Andison (New York: Philosophical Library, 1946), p. 162.

4. *Ibid.*

5. Rationalism holds that reason, which exists in all men, enables a man without any further moral or spiritual qualifications to distinguish between truth and falsity. Truth is something that can be appealed to universally; it is something that can be discovered and agreed upon

rationally. But, as I shall seek to demonstrate later, there must be a fundamental change in our ordinary moral-intellectual consciousness before we are capable of apprehending Truth.

6. Walter Kaufmann, *Existentialism from Dostoevsky to Sartre* (New York: Meridian Books, 1956), p. 11. Kaufmann is of course correct in pointing out that there is a considerable lack of agreement among existential thinkers. Originally Existentialism (although at the time not called by that name) was "religious" in its orientation (as in Pascal and Kierkegaard), but later some of its spokesmen were outspoken atheists (Sartre). Methodologically some of the existentialists have followed closely Husserl's phenomenology while others have adhered to more traditional kinds of intellectual analysis. Some existentialists (Heidegger) have sought to construct a new ontology, a new approach to the problem of being; others (Jaspers) have denied the possibility of such an ontology and would restrict Existentialism to a philosophical anthropology. Marcel, with his doctrines of participation and encounter, works within the framework of a Catholic *Weltanschauung*, while Sartre, as indicated, denies the validity of any religious transcendence. Still, as suggested by F. H. Heinemann (*Existentialism and the Modern Predicament*), there is a common enough attitude and method among the leading existential thinkers to bring them together, especially for the purpose of contrasting them with other possible attitudes and methods.

7. James Collins points out that, for Kierkegaard, "without the passional factor, especially will, there is no way of advancing from the dreamy, esthetic state to the moral and religious phases of existence. It is not voluntarism [romantic naturalism] but an honest attempt to see man steadily and in his actual dynamism which prompts this emphasis upon other powers than reason." (*The Existentialists* [Chicago: Henry Regnery Co., 1952], p. 8)

8. Kierkegaard, *Concluding Unscientific Postscript*, trans. D. F. Swenson and W. Laurie (Princeton: Princeton University Press, 1941), bk. 2, pt. 2, chap. 2, p. 182.

9. See Kierkegaard, *Fear and Trembling*.

10. See Sartre's major philosophical work, *L'être et le neant* (*Being and Nothingness*).

11. The difference between the problem of communication in Existentialism and in a spiritual metaphysics is that between communicating the contents of the irrational phenomena which one encounters in the shadowy recesses of one's personal subjective being and the infinite joy, knowledge, and life which one experiences in the vital depth of

creative being; in other words, it is the difference between communicating *the situation of one's self* and communicating *the reality of the
Self.*

12. Jacques Maritain, in his critique of Existentialism, writes: "What reveals
subjectivity to itself is not an irrational break (however profound and
gratuitous it may be) in an irrational flow of moral and psychological
phenomena, of dreams, automatisms, urges, and images surging up-
wards from the unconscious. Neither is it the anguish of forced choice.
It is self-mastery for the purpose of self-giving." (*Existence and the
Existent*, trans. Lewis Galantiere and Gerald B. Phelan [New York:
Pantheon Books, 1948], p. 89)
Maritain also rightly points out that "such philosophies are in reality
philosophies of action, either *praxis* and the transforming action of the
world, or of moral creation *a nihilo* and liberty for liberty's sake. This
is why the very notion of contemplation has become unthinkable for
them, and they have no other resource than, in the fine scorn of
ignorance, to stigmatise with the name of 'quietism' the highest and
purest activity of the intellect . . . ." (*Ibid.*, p. 141)

13. By the Christian view of man I refer primarily to its "Protestant form"
as this is grounded in the Pauline-Augustinian side of Christianity.
The "Catholic view" of man, as articulated in medieval thought, is by
and large a combination of Greek rationalism and Biblical supernatu-
ralism. It developed (e.g., in St. Thomas Aquinas) into a rational-
humanism and, with the possible exception of its eschatology, offers
few significant points which are not already involved in the views of
man which I am considering.

14. *De civitate Dei*, bk. XII, chap. 6.

15. *The Dhammapada* I. 1.

16. *Bhagavadgītā* XVII. 3.

17. *To the Thessalonians*, I, (chap. 4, verse 8).

18. *The Essence of Christianity*, trans. George Eliot (New York: Harper
& Bros., 1957), p. 62.

19. Reinhold Niebuhr, *The Nature and Destiny of Man*, 2 vols. (New
York: Charles Scribner's Sons, 1951), 2:49.

20. *Ibid.*, 1:201.

21. Etienne Gilson, *The Mystical Theology of St. Bernard*, trans. A. H. C.
Downes (London: Sheed & Ward, 1940), p. 120.

THE ABSOLUTE AS BEING

1. The statement, "the Absolute assumes being," is not intended to mean
that every thing *qua* thing may be identified with the Divine; rather,

it intends to set forth the notion that the basic features of being are not-different from the Absolute in this its status as being. The Absolute, according to our understanding, is not an extra-cosmic personal being; rather, it is the very fullness of existence, and although it is veiled by our habitual sense-and-mental experience and is indeterminate to our finite language and reason, it must in its status as being be seen as not-other than the primal structures of the mind and all existence.

2. For Hegel, on the other hand, who represents another side of the idealistic tradition, categories are the basic stuff of the evolution or unfolding of pure thought. The categories comprise all the fundamental philosophical notions—be they in logic, ethics, epistemology, etc.—which develop in an absolute scheme of rational order. All categories, according to Hegel, are exhibited in the order from which they arise in thought.

3. For both Kant and Hegel, man's mind at the stage of its highest rational self-consciousness is ultimately the very center of existence. Nature, in the final analysis (and as summed up by Schopenhauer) is only a *Vorstellung*—a "representation." This extreme (egotistic) sundering of man from Nature, however, simply does not correspond with our many-sided awareness, even in ordinary experience, of our dynamic interrelatedness with Nature. And the same difficulty holds with other forms of one-level idealism as well. Berkeley, for example, with his *esse est percipi*, was called upon to introduce a transcendent deity (as a kind of *deus ex machina*) in order to bring some measure of order into an otherwise hopelessly relativistic and perhaps solipsistic world.

CATEGORIES OF BEING

1. It was one of the great discoveries of classical Chinese culture that a spiritual life which is entirely *natural* is expressed in a subtle rhythm of being. This is clearly exemplified in the first of Hsieh Ho's famous "six canons" on art, which were set down in the fourth century. The canon states that the embodiment of a rhythmic vitality, expressive of the movement of life, is necessary for all great art (*ch'i-yun sheng-tung*). Benjamin Rowland explains it nicely this way: "By this [canon] the chief aim of the artist was to imbue his painted forms with the feeling of vitality or spirit-harmony in accordance with the special kind of movement, rhythm, or life characteristic of all things in the world of nature" (*Art in East and West* [Cambridge: Harvard University Press, 1965], p. 20). The artist was to identify himself so completely with this rhythmic vitality that it became a part of him and

consequently was directly embodied in his work. According to Wang Wei: "The wind rises from the green forest, and foaming water rushes in the stream. Alas! Such painting cannot be achieved by the physical movements of the fingers and the hand, but only by the spirit entering into them. This is the nature of painting." (*Li-tai ming-hua chi,* 6:5b-6b, in *The Sources of Chinese Tradition,* ed. Wm. Theodore deBary et al. [New York: Columbia University Press, 1960], p. 295)

2. The mechanical routine imposed upon so many of us in modern industrialized societies represents precisely that distortion of a natural rhythm which does violence to the integrity of an individual. By compelling us to respond to and adjust to sequences of movement and action that are determined primarily by a criterion of "efficiency," our work patterns (and oftentimes our leisure ones as well) only enslave us.

3. *Summa theologiae* I, q. 5, a. 4, ad. 1.

4. Jacques Maritain, for example, who closely follows the *id quod visum placet* aesthetics of Thomas, writes: "If beauty delights the mind, it is because beauty is essentially a certain excellence or perfection in the proportion of things to the mind" (*Art and Scholasticism,* trans. J. F. Scanlan [New York: Charles Scribner's Sons, 1954], p. 20).

5. The category of "integrity" perhaps underlies the famous teaching of the "doctrine of the mean" (*chung-yung*) in early Confucianism and is given its most prominent role in that tradition. According to the doctrine of the mean, all action can be made harmonious by ordering one's inner life according to a principle of sincerity (*ch'eng*). Ch'eng is the active fulfillment of "human naturalness" (*jen*). "Sincerity means the completion of the self, and the Way is self-directing. Sincerity is the beginning and end of things. Without sincerity there would be nothing.... Sincerity is not only the completion of one's own self, it is that by which all things are completed." ("The Doctrine of the Mean," sec. 25, in *A Source Book of Chinese Philosophy,* trans. and comp. Wing-tsit Chan [Princeton: Princeton University Press, 1963], p. 108)

6. Feeling, it is quite clear, is not to be confounded with mere passion or emotion. The latter, one might say, is the former become distorted and groundless. Feeling is rooted in being and imparts power and direction to the mind just insofar as it is an expression of being. Passion is usually the radical distortion of rhythm, proportion, and integrity; it tends to be fragmented; it lacks a sense of fitness and harmony; it overcomes rather than meets the "relational other" of experience.

7. In a later section (chap. 8) an attempt will be made to set forth a structure of "purpose" in the broader terms of actual human develop-

ment. I will try to show there that the most fundamental purposes that inform human activity are those by which we seek to individualize, to universalize, and to dissolve our phenomenal selves.

8. It is an inveterate habit of our mind to take its features, as these are discerned in our habitual sense-mental consciousness, as the general terms of being, and to read everything in nature according to them. But our normal level of consciousness is a limited one and, as I shall seek to demonstrate later, is a "diverted" one; that is to say, it is not in actuality what it is in essentiality, an unlimited power of awareness. A simple introspective, functional, or behaviorist psychology teaches us that purpose, in the limited sense of a directed social selectivity, is a general characteristic of human consciousness. Not resting content with this basic fact, however, we then read this purpose into Nature and impose a teleology upon it—believing that there is some hidden purpose, meaning, or end in life. But as modern science has shown, there are no "final causes" in Nature, i.e., it is impossible to determine any ultimate ends toward which nature strives. This denial of "final causes," however, ought not to be construed as a denial of spiritual or purposeless-purpose. When we seek to guide our lives in conformity with the principles of the spirit, we find that selective purposiveness, the selecting of certain ends and the movement towards their attainment, no longer holds as a feature of consciousness. In the spirit one is confronted with a glorious simplicity and disinterestedness; consciousness here simply extends and encompasses being.

9. Aristotle *De memoria et reminiscentia*, chap. 1, 449b. 29.

10. Plotinus *Enneads* (trans. Stephen MacKenna) IV. 3. 25. Bergson, the grand master of memory, bears this out when he notes that "without that survival of the past in the present [through memory] there would be no duration but only instantaneity" ("Introduction to Metaphysics," in *The Creative Mind*, trans. Mabelle L. Andison [New York: Philosophical Library, 1946], p. 179).

11. St. John of the Cross, *Ascent of Mount Carmel*, trans. E. Allison Peers (New York: Doubleday & Co., Image Books, n.d.), bk. III, chap. 5, p. 277.

12. I am dealing here with memory in metaphysical not psychological terms; that is, I am seeking to determine the meaning and status of memory as a feature of being. The place of memory as it functions psychologically in our ordinary sense-mental experience will be taken up at a later point.

13. Plato, in his doctrine of recollection (*anamnesis*), held that the mind of man contains various innate rational powers and essential forms of knowledge, and that these can be brought to waking consciousness through a kind of rational dialectic (see *Meno*). The Platonic memory

is bound up with time, in the usual sense of successiveness, as its content is individual principles; but all events are present to memory in its primary status essentially, and no events are viewed by it actually. This means that in the fullness of memory nothing is seen in its separativeness as a concrete actuality bound up with past, present, and future, in the way that we ordinarily view and review the transient events of our lives and of history, but that everything is seen in its essential interrelatedness. In short, the fullness of memory operates only in the fullness of time, not in time as succession.

It is also tempting to seek a correlation between this depth of memory discovered in spiritual experience and the extraordinary capacities for memory that psychology has discovered to be present in man. Through various means (e.g., hypnosis) it has been discovered that a man can recall a large number of facts, situations, and reactions which ordinarily he is unable to recall. But it would be misleading to establish this correlation for the simple reason that the true depth of memory and extraordinary capacities of memory that are bound up in time still occur on different levels of being.

14. Philosophers and psychologists, for the most part, tend to consider memory only in its most universal terms and thus neglect the many interesting subtleties that are present in our memory-functioning. For example, the memories which we have of experiences that have been shared with others have very often an entirely different emotional quality and clarity from those of the same things experienced when alone. And in terms of strictly subjective experiences one finds there a peculiar relation between desire and memory. How often does one experience something—perhaps while watching a sunset, while walking in the woods in autumn—which awakens a kind of intense, poignant desire for some sort of indeterminate past experience? One suddenly feels a keen desire to possess this present experience in the full way which one's memory hints that one has experienced before—and immediately on becoming aware of this desire, the memory disappears.

One of the first things that one is called upon to rid oneself of in the following of a spiritual path to self-realization is one's memories. In any extended period of solitude one tends to take a lengthy review of one's life, and not always voluntarily, rather on the contrary, memories seem to surge up within one and are repressed or cast out only with a great effort. Memories sometimes are as unwanted intruders. They have not been invited and they refuse to leave.

15. This criticism would seem to apply equally to the Confucian tradition of Chinese thought which, like the Greek, maintained that there is an

ideal form of human being which is present in man's nature and has only to be brought forth and made vital in experience. The ideal pattern for man is called *jen*—variously translated as "human heartedness," "perfect virtue," "humanity," "benevolent love," "true manhood," etc.—the Chinese character consisting of the character for 'a man' and the character for 'two,' suggesting thereby the actuality of man as a being in society. But the concept of *jen* fails, it seems, to do justice to the complexities of the category of the ideal in experience and tends to make of the human ideal itself something fixed and determined (as exemplified in *li*, the rules for "propriety").

16. D. W. Gotshalk, "Form," in *The Problems of Aesthetics*, ed. Eliseo Vivas and Murray Krieger (New York: Rinehart & Co., 1953), pp. 198–199.

17. It is possible that Spinoza worked with this meaning of the term in his doctrine that there is within man a tendency to react to all the changes and forces that affect him in such a way that he maintains a unity, an equilibrium natural to himself. (Spinoza calls this inherent tendency to maintain equilibrium *conatus*.) Whenever one interacts with something or someone else there is the likelihood that a disruption of one's surface integration will occur; and hence, to overcome this one must seek to stabilize oneself on a deeper level. According to Spinoza, there is freedom only in this deeper equilibrium. One is free from the tyranny of one's elemental, passional nature only when one is stabilized within one's true center of being. When one has realized the depth of equilibrium, one is whole.

18. Henri Bergson, *Creative Evolution*, trans. Arthur Mitchell (New York: Random House, 1944), p. 179.

19. A. N. Whitehead writes that "the extensive continuity of the physical universe has usually been construed to mean that there is a continuity of becoming. But if we admit that 'something becomes,' it is easy, by employing Zeno's method, to prove that there can be no continuity of becoming. There is a becoming of continuity, but no continuity of becoming." (*Process and Reality* [New York: Macmillan Co., 1929], p. 53.) This may be true verbally for the "extensive continuity of the physical universe" but it is not true for the subsistent structure of being. In the Absolute, a "becoming of continuity" and the "continuity of becoming" mutually involve one another and mean fundamentally the same thing.

20. Plotinus *Enneads* III. 7. 7.

21. Kant, *Critique of Pure Reason*, trans. Norman Kemp Smith, 2d ed. (London: Macmillan & Co., 1950), pp. 71, 77.

22. Aristotle writes: "We apprehend time only when we have marked

motion, marking it by 'before' and 'after'; and it is only when we have perceived 'before' and 'after' in motion that we say that time has elapsed" (*Physics* bk. IV, chap. 11, 219a: 25). What Aristotle seems to be saying is that where there is no "motion," no change, there is no *apprehension* of time. We would say that our sense of time is very much dependent upon the form of consciousness by and through which we apprehend the world. The further we advance in the development of consciousness the less does time with its 'before' and 'after' maintain a hold upon us.

23. According to Kant, with whom our position here might be confused, the *a priori* is that aspect of knowledge which has a non-empirical validity. The content of knowledge is given by experience, the form of knowledge, its apriority, is provided by the knowing human mind. Kant, however, failed to see that consciousness has levels, and that the *a priori* in consciousness is a manifestation of a categorical status which transcends our ordinary sense-mental knowing. Further, he failed to see that the categories are not altogether fixed and stable, but are themselves developmental. The categories of understanding in their existent status are basically formal, that is to say, empty of specific content, and are thus open to progressive development in terms of the contents that they embrace and in terms of various patterns of social conditioning. Space-time is an existent capacity to order simple happenings into "events"—to recognize some kind of spatial-temporal regularity; but the category does not prescribe any specific way of ordering happenings. (And hence, in this analysis, we need not get involved in the problems raised by Kant's assumption of Euclidian geometry as *the* structure of space. No particular geometry, as translated into a physical description, need be specified.) When it is said, then, that space-time is a form of the understanding it is meant that space-time is a structural feature of consciousness that is present in all experience. In its existent and developmental statuses space-time is not so much a necessary condition for knowledge, one which insures the validity of the content of certain principles of thought, as it is simply a form in terms of which consciousness is cognitive. All men of healthy consciousness have a capacity to recognize space-time, i.e., to organize experience according to spatial-temporal determinations, and each man, at any given time, has a somewhat different spatial-temporal complex forming his consciousness.

24. Strictly speaking we do not, of course, perceive time directly; we perceive things in terms of time. The common experience of our being able to determine how much time has passed (and often with amazing accuracy) without our having looked at a watch or clock is explainable

in terms of our having internalized a mode of measurement. We say an hour and a half has passed, or it must now be around a quarter to eight; we are aware normally of time as structured and made objective by us in terms of regulated measurement, and this awareness persists even when we are shut off, for short periods, from the instruments that determine our temporal awareness. We continue to order experience by this internalized measurement and we become aware of the measurement itself in the absence of events. Another way of putting it would be to say that time is not a fact of the empirical world *per se*; rather it is one of the conditions by which we determine the facts of the world. And, further, this determination is itself apparently subject to cultural conditions. In experiments dealing with optical illusions in different cultures, it was shown that certain non-Westerners were, for example, less susceptible to the Müller-Lyer illusion ($>\!\!-\!\!-\!\!-\!\!<$, $\longleftarrow\longrightarrow$) than were Westerners, with the conclusion being drawn that "the perception of space involves, to an important extent, the acquisition of habits of perceptual inference" (Marshall H. Segall, Donald T. Campbell, and Melville J. Herskovits, "Cultural Differences in the Perception of Geometric Illusions," *Science* 139 [1963]:769).

25. In aesthetics, for example, it is common to distinguish between those arts within which space-time is a formal element or indigenous constituent in the work and those where it is only its general context. Music as compared to classic sculpture not only occurs within a general space-time context, it necessarily employs space-time as a vital element in its construction. The rhythms and harmonies, the modulations of music use space-time and are part and parcel of it. The same is true, in a somewhat different way, with poetry and literature. The literary imagination freely juxtaposes spatial-temporal elements in the construction of its action; it moves freely according to its own aesthetic laws from one time and place to another. This free use of various space-time situations demonstrates clearly that our ordinary awareness of space-time as a definite external sequential continuum is not a rigid ultimate, for it can, with varying degrees, be dispensed with.

26. The notion that our common-sense idea of time, with its sequential past, present, and future, as measured by clocks, is but one status of the space-time category has come to mean for much of modern science and philosophy that space-time is just a mental construct. It is clearly recognized that if time is measured by motion and motion is measured by time, then time itself is *defined* operationally in terms of various modes of measurement. Augustine's analysis of time as subjective (see *Confessions*, bk. 11) has won out, as it were, over Aristotle, and to-

gether with relativity theory has displaced Newton's absolute time. The outcome of this, however, has been more to dissolve the independent phenomenal reality of time than to understand it categorically. Most modern analyses of time still fail to see that durational time can be understood only by its relation to "eternity"; that the category of time must be seen as a multi-leveled category and not simply in a one-level phenomenal status.

27. The failure to appreciate this multi-dimensional character of space-time is in no small measure responsible for much of the confusion in traditional metaphysics. When reasoning about time from the empirical level of events (as measured, anticipated, responded to) is extended to a pure conceptual, metaphysical level we have all the puzzles that the linguistic analyst delights in dissolving. The puzzles indeed arise from a kind of category confusion, namely, that of confounding or failing to distinguish between levels of experience. The "common language philosopher" who is determined to confine his analysis to ordinary language, although he avoids the category mistakes of the typical rationalist, is not, however, able to offer much in the way of understanding. By insisting that "if anyone is able to use the word ['time'] correctly, in all sorts of contexts and on the right sort of occasions, he knows 'what time is' and no formula in the world can make him wiser" the analyst merely avoids the issue. He is saying simply that there is nothing to understand (for after all any young child can learn to use words "correctly"). (See Freidrich Waismann, "Analytic-Synthetic," *Analysis*, nos. 2, 3 [December 1950, January 1951]).

28. *Die Bestimmung des Menschen* II. 177. 23.

29. Fung Yu-Lan, *A Short History of Chinese Philosophy* (New York: Macmillan Co., 1960), p. 222.

The doctrine of "internal relations" asserts, then, "that everything, if we knew enough, would turn out to be internally related to everything else" (Brand Blanshard, *The Nature of Thought*, 2 vols. [New York: Macmillan Co., 1941], 2:451). The doctrine of "external relations," on the other hand, which is most often contrasted with it, holds that relations are entirely of a formal nature and do not affect the terms which belong to it. Blanshard summarizes the difference neatly when stating: "A relation is internal to a term when in its absence the term would be different; it is external when its addition or withdrawal would make *no* difference to the term" (*Ibid.*). Cf. Bertrand Russell, *An Inquiry into Meaning and Truth*, for a concise exposition and defense of the "external relations" doctrine, and for an enumeration of various formal relations, such as transitive, symmetrical, etc., which the logical counterpart of this doctrine recognizes.

30. Various attempts have indeed been made in philosophy to assert the full reality of universals without reference to the Absolute, but since at least the time of Hegel the traditional realist positions, let alone any attempt to demonstrate them, have become unintelligible to most philosophers. The Platonic doctrine, especially in its medieval form (prior to the Aristotelian renaissance of the thirteenth century), which held that universals (the Ideas) were perfect forms that existed apart from the individuals that instantiate them, and also the Aristotelian "moderate realism," which held that although universals are found only in things (*in rebus*) they are nevertheless completely real, have been quite thoroughly rejected in favor of a straightforward empiricist analysis of how universals originate from sense-experience and function in cognitive consciousness. William of Occam's old nominalism—that universals come after things in the mind of man and do not correspond to anything real outside of themselves—has essentially won the day.

31. See Max Planck, "The Concept of Causality in Physics," trans. Frank Gaynor, in *Scientific Autobiography and Other Papers* (New York: Philosophical Library, 1949). Planck, in this paper, goes on to make a distinction—reminiscent of the old scholastic distinction between *causa cognoscendi*, the reason for affirming a truth, and *causa existendi*, the cause of an occurrence or event—between causality as it applies to the interaction of theoretical concepts and as it applies to phenomenal events.

   The equating of causation with necessity or certainty was prevalent generally in the seventeenth century. The philosophy of this time (e.g., Descartes, Spinoza) held to a rigid determinism in nature. The world was looked upon as a mechanistic order of efficient causality, an order which admits of no exceptions. In the seventeenth century Leibniz is perhaps the outstanding exception with respect to the mechanistic view of causality. According to Leibniz, all efficient causes can be reduced to final causes in the form of an "immanent causality." That is, each simple substance or "monad" may be said to contain within itself the causes for all its subsequent states; each monad possesses the capacity to generate out of itself the entire phenomena associated with it. It was for the eighteenth century to bring causation inward. British empiricism gave to causation a psychological status. Hume, for example, held that causality is a habit of the mind; it is the habit of seeing and thereby expecting always to find a certain constant conjunction obtaining between events. Kant, who (according to his testimony) was awakened from his slumbers by Hume, held on the other hand that causality is an *a priori* form of the understanding. It is only through the presupposition of causation that appearances may be ordered and comprehended in a systematic unity. And causation, for Kant, applies not merely to our ideas about events, but to events themselves.

In more recent times, with the growth of the sciences, causation has come to be regarded in a less inward way as the observation of regular sequences under various known conditions. Further, within modern science there is the tendency to replace the idea of necessary causation with that of probability. Rationalists have always held that necessitation means implication (that if a cause is given, the effect necessarily follows); empiricists have held that necessitation means observed conformity of conjunction; the modern *statistical* orientation holds that causation, that is, a statistical law, represents a temporary equilibrium among forces which permit of *prediction*. There have been many different attempts to interpret the precise meaning of the probability factor present in statistical formulations of causal processes. Some have held for the "relative frequency view," which states that probability means the relative frequency that a certain event will occur in a given class of events; others hold to the "degree of confirmation view," which states that probability is essentially a logical concept which is concerned with the degree to which a hypothesis is confirmed by its empirical evidence, and so on. See R. von Mies, *Positivism*, chaps. 13 and 14; Phillip Frank, *Modern Science and Its Philosophy*, chap. 1; Bertrand Russell, *Human Knowledge*, chap. 1, pt. 4; Rudolph Carnap, *Logical Foundations of Probability*, chap. 4.

32. The non-rational conditioning relation also may help one to understand the "way" to spiritual experience—or why one cannot put forward a way that can guarantee decisive results. Spiritual life, as many discover, is not subject to some kind of rigid necessity. No amount of mere method is sufficient in itself to bring one to spiritual realization, for the life of spirit cannot be mechanical: if the fulfillment of a series of steps or a set of conditions could with certainty produce a given effect, then that effect would be part of the causal series, and if the effect were spiritual realization (a state of being different in kind from empirical experience) then it would be self-contradictory to see it as resulting from a set of sufficient conditions.

33. The question is often raised as to whether there is some core meaning to "causality" which has endured in man's thinking processes from primitive to modern times and which thus makes possible the asserting of it in categorical form. In primitive thought, causality is generally conceived of as the relation between various events that immediately affect one's life, with the events being directed by some hidden power

which may itself be subject to human placation. In Greek thought (e.g., Aristotle), on the other hand, causality was regarded as the total process by which something is brought into being and constituted. "Formal" and "final," as well as "efficient" and "material" causes were thus recognized. Between these interpretations and modern mechanistic and statistical ones, there would seem to be an enormous gap. However, in all cases, in its most basic elementary form causality is conceived of as some kind of ordering relation between empirical events viewed sequentially. Necessarily we read some principle of change into nature, for without that principle, apart from the fact that sense-mental experience testifies to regularities, we would find life to be entirely precarious, and hence unendurable.

If we turn to Asian thought we also find various ways of thinking about causality which tend to support the claim about its universality. Although the Chinese gave little consideration to the problems of causality with which we are familiar, we find nevertheless that they had a keen awareness of the presence of ordering relations in the world of change. The archetypal models of the *I Ching*, the five agents of classifications, the *yin/yang* dialectic, all clearly point to this awareness. Instead of a linear direction in causal series, we have cyclical movement; instead of a recognition of discrete events, we have a mutual involvement or "interpenetration" between them. In the appendices to the *I Ching*, for example, we find that "between Heaven and Earth nothing goes away that does not return," and "when there is end, there is beginning," etc. See Fung Yu-Lan, *A History of Chinese Philosophy*, 2 vols., trans. Derk Bodde (Princeton: Princeton University Press, 1952), 1:378–395.

In the Indian tradition problems of causality are extensively treated and a doctrine of causality often occupies a central place in a given system—e.g., the *pariṇāmavāda* (the theory of the transformation of a cause into a pre-existing effect) of the Sāṁkhya; the *pratītyasamutpāda*, or "law of dependent origination," in Buddhism; the *vivartavāda* (theory of the appearance-only status of the effect) in Advaita Vedānta. With the possible exceptions of Buddhism and the Nyāya system most of the Indian argument on causality is primarily concerned with cosmic change—how is it that one thing or domain of Nature comes from another thing or order of being. And for all Indian systems, in greater or lesser degree, we find a causal ordering of human action in the doctrine of *karman*—that every act reverberates back into the actor and conditions his being.

34. Since the rise of the various biological and social sciences, it is customary to view man more or less completely in terms of causation—

as he is a *product* of various social, hereditary, environmental influ-
ences. This reduction of man to causation is very much in error insofar as it denies all that is of true value in man, namely the spiritual
levels of his being. (See critique of "scientific naturalism" in chapter
3.) This reductive orientation nevertheless has done much to enable us
to understand those aspects of our nature which are subject to causation; it permits us to enter directly into the causal process within ourselves and to alter it when it is destructive (e.g., the impressive accom-
plishments of various psychoanalytic techniques to restore health to
persons suffering from serious emotional and mental disturbances).
However, just as causality is a dimension in any work of art (manifest
in the process in which it has come into being), but the work as a
whole transcends it (that is, cannot be understood or appreciated
solely in terms of it), so causality is manifest in man as a dimension
of his being, but he cannot be reduced to it. Causality, in actuality, is
applicable to man only when certain aspects of his nature are taken in
isolation.

35. According to Heisenberg, "the interaction between observer and object
[in sub-atomic processes] causes uncontrollable and large changes in
the system being observed, because of the discontinuous character of
atomic processes. The immediate consequence of this circumstance is
that in general every experiment performed to determine some nu-
merical quantity renders the knowledge of others illusory, since the
uncontrollable perturbation of the observed system alters the values of
previously determined quantities." (*The Physical Principles of Quantum Theory*, as quoted by Ernest Nagel in *Freedom and Reason*
[Glencoe: Free Press, 1951].)

36. I have not been concerned here with analyzing or adopting a position
on the many epistemological questions about causality—e.g., its status
as a possible heuristic principle, the adequacy of the language of
necessary and sufficient conditions, etc. These problems are of vital
philosophical interest, but, for purposes of understanding the categorical status of causality, they may conveniently be put aside. From this
analysis I conclude only that "causality" is multi-leveled in our experience: that like the other categories, it has its subsistent quality, its
universal presence in understanding, its development feature in all
experience.

MAN AS A DIVERTED BEING

1. I am not suggesting that the order which is a quality of the soul actually becomes our empirical mind, rather, I am trying to understand
the way in which our empirical mind actually functions in terms of

various needs. The essential structure of mind and its "actuality" are different things; they are on different levels of being. The natural biological explanation of the mind as a product of evolutionary factors may be accepted on the level of mind to which it pertains. In actuality, the distinctive characteristics of the mind do seem to follow from the needs of the organism to adapt to and to master its natural environment, with the habitual functions of the mind reflecting these and other needs. Philosophers who tend to accept the broad evolutionary hypothesis, however, seldom carry its implications through to their proper conclusion. They still like to hold to the possibility that the empirical mind can be a truth-seeking or truth-revealing mind largely along traditional rationalistic lines. One should however accept these limitations of the empirical mind to their full measure and insist that it is only when the mind moves to a deeper level of its being, only when habitual natural needs are overcome, that one can speak of a genuine truth-seeking or truth-revealing power of the mind.

2. The law of contradiction is not of course to be accounted for solely in terms of an "aesthetic need"; for indeed it rests upon many other considerations—e.g., it seems to be indispensable for the constructing of any kind of systematic body of propositional truth.

3. This difference between artificial order and authentic order is clearly recognizable in art. One can distinguish between those formative processes which reflect an essential spirituality of order from those which are the result of the formal needs of the intellect. If we compare, for example, a late Turner or a typical southern Sung painting with a typical High Renaissance work (Giorgone, Titian) or with a Poussin, we see at once that the former is striving to express an inner harmony of nature while the latter is striving to impose an order upon nature which will appeal to our "aesthetic of the reason." The Renaissance or neo-classical artist did not seek to reflect the spiritual order in being, but to substitute a rational one of his own. Whenever one takes one's own ordered products as substitutes for, rather than as symbols of, spiritual order, necessarily they are the products of diversion.

4. One must insist upon this rather strongly today, for with the development of so many "irrationalist" tendencies in modern thought and culture, it is often argued, in a very peculiar way, that what the intellect is unable to accomplish in providing us with an understanding of our world can be accomplished by a sole reliance upon some kind of anti-intellectual unthinking commitment to reformative action.

5. This destructive principle of the will is similar, phenomenologically, in many respects to what Freud called an "aggressive instinct." (Cf. especially his *Beyond the Pleasure Principle*.) It differs from the Freudian

concept, however, primarily in that it is not regarded as something ineradicable in man's nature, and hence it is not a cause for maintaining a deep pessimism with respect to human nature. The destructive principle of the will is regarded as only a part of a general diversion process. Admittedly, the "re-diversion" or "re-birth" necessary for spiritual life is an extremely difficult task; but it is possible to man and is indeed necessary if he is to fulfill his destiny as man. Freud is right, however, in finding little to rejoice about in those aspects of man's experience when, through whatever circumstances, he is enabled to give an uncontrolled release to his destructive energies; their release becomes the most blatant denial of the spiritual in man.

6. Again, a comparison with Freud: during several phases of his work in which he attempted to set forth a "topology" of mental behavior, Freud asserted the domain of what he called the "superego." The superego is the "place" where the demands of social behavior are internalized and serve as a brake to other (generally asocial) energies. The rules given by one's parents, the moral codes of the groups to which one belongs, the values of the society within which one lives, all become written into one's psyche and limit one's conscious desires. The superego was thus conceived of as a force overlooking and restraining the ego. The id seeks self-gratification; the superego through the agency of the ego tells it which forms are acceptable and which unacceptable. Within my analysis, "image" and "fear" serve primarily the same role—only rather than regarding them as separate domains of the "psyche," I regard them as fundamental constituents of our empirical will, as they are part and parcel of all volitional activity.

7. *The World as Will and Idea*, bk. IV, sec. 57. Unfortunately the only "salvation" that Schopenhauer could discover for this predicament was that of an unself-conscious aesthetic contemplation: the freeing of the self from the will entirely. However, when once our ordinary human will is understood as it represents a diversion of something deeper into a need, other more efficacious "salvations" are possible; namely, the re-diversion of that will in conformation to the nature of our higher eternal will—and the reflection of that conformation in all other activities.

8. The diversion of our nature, however, is not temporal in the sense that it can be determined chronologically within a given person's life development. The history of self-development is certainly not one of a simple movement from childlike purity to the complexities characteristic of adulthood. The will of a child, for example, is far from "pure." Basically it is just as diverted as is that of the adult—and, in a sense, more so, for the partial control of the will through reasoned judgment comes about only with a certain maturity.

MAN'S CONSTRUCTION OF A HABITUAL REALITY

1. For a brief description of "perception" in Vedānta, see, for example, my *Advaita Vedānta: A Philosophical Reconstruction* (Honolulu: East-West Center Press, 1969), pp. 90–92.
2. Max Wertheimer, "Gestalt Theory," in *A Source Book of Gestalt Psychology*, prepared by Willis D. Ellis (London: Routledge & Kegan Paul, 1950), p. 2.
3. Wolfgang Köhler, "Physical Gestalten," in *A Source Book of Gestalt Psychology*, p. 17.
4. Wolfgang Köhler, *The Place of Value in a World of Fact* (New York: Liveright Publishing Corp., 1938), p. 85.
5. Cf. Bruno Petermann, *The Gestalt Theory and the Problem of Configuration* (New York: Harcourt, Brace & Co., 1932), pp. 110 ff.
6. Kurt Koffka writes that the "correspondence between phenomenal and real things is, according to our theory, not primarily a matter of experience—although we do not deny that experience may influence thing properties—but the direct result of organization. Psychophysically, the process distributions which correspond to perceived things must in several respects be similar to physical things, and therefore we must, on the basis of isomorphism, conclude that behavioral things have autochtonously characteristics similar to real things." (*Principles of Gestalt Psychology*, [New York: Harcourt, Brace & Co., 1935], p. 305)
   See also Petermann, *op. cit.*, pp. 40, 56–58, and especially p. 297, where he points out that "an autochtonous ontological reality is attributed to the gestalt as such. . . . The gestalten thus become primary realities, existential ultimates . . . ."
7. Gardner Murphy, "Gestalt and Field Theory," in *Readings in the Philosophy of Science*, ed. P. Weiner (New York: Charles Scribner's Sons, 1935), p. 212.
8. Floyd H. Allport, *Theories of Perception and the Concept of Structure* (New York: John Wiley & Sons, 1955), p. 115.
   Among the basic laws of perception established by gestalt psychology are: (1) the law of closed form (a form always tends to complete itself); (2) the law of pregnancy (parts tend to organize themselves into units as "good" as the circumstances permit); (3) the law of proximity (elements closest to each other tend to form units); (4) the law of similarity (elements which are similar to one another in size, shape, color tend to form units); (5) the law of common movement (elements which have similar direction tend to be grouped together).
9. And hence in contradistinction to Kurt Koffka's statement that "we claim that every gestalt [as objective form] has order and meaning, of

however low or high a degree, and that for a gestalt quantity and quality are the same" (*Principles of Gestalt Psychology*, p. 22).

10. Koffka and other gestaltists certainly recognize that a gestalt is organized in time (*ibid.*, pp. 424–464), but nevertheless most of the descriptions of perception found in gestalt literature minimize or tend to neglect this simple fact.

11. The general *description* which is arrived at here is not intended as an adequate *explanation* of perception. It is my intention only to point out certain factors that seem to be insufficiently dealt with by gestalt theory, and this for the purpose of tracing some philosophical implications of the theory.

12. Josiah Royce brings this out very clearly when he writes: "It is not true that we merely find outer objects as independent of our will. . . . We find them possessed of characters only in so far as we ourselves co-operate in the construction, in the definition, in the linkage of these very predicates, which we then ascribe to the object. Since to be sure, our *need* of thus defining objects is given to us . . . in order to relieve our need, we are constrained to define our object thus and thus. . . . If you have no interest in the object, its supposed independence of your will can impose upon you no recognition of this its barely external nature. You observe what you need to be observed." ("The External and the Practical," *Philosophical Review* 13 (1904):113–142)

13. There is perhaps no theme or area of study in psychology, other than perception itself, which has been as enduring and perplexing as that of "memory." Everyone recognizes the tremendous role that it plays in experience, but no one seems to know just what it is. In fact, whether memory is an "it" at all is highly questionable. Koffka, for example, states that "memory is but a word which labels a great number of different achievements without explaining them" (*Principles of Gestalt Psychology*, p. 424). Within psychology as such one need have no quarrel with this; I am seeking only to point to that functional power of consciousness—describe it as one can, call it what one will—that provides one with the disposition to impute a meaning, a body of interpretation, to a selected perceived form. Consciousness is creative in its conceptual ordering of experience. Not only does it go outward, as it were, to embrace the form of the object, it gives to the object the richness of its experience in the world. And some kind of recall of past experience is unquestionably a functional part of that creativity. The gestaltists, of course, do not deny this; they maintain that past experience is introduced into perception only as a function of gestalt organization. The structure of the perceptual field determines what aspects of past experience are utilized.

14. *Language and Myth*, trans. Susanne K. Langer (New York: Dover Publications, n.d.), p. 28.

15. Ernst Cassirer has also rightly pointed out that "we can apprehend a spatial 'whole' only by presupposing the formation of various temporal series: even though the simultaneous synthesis of consciousness constitutes a specific and original part of consciousness in general, it can only be completed and represented on the basis of the successive synthesis" (*The Philosophy of Symbolic Forms*, 3 vols., trans. Ralph Manheim [New Haven: Yale University Press, 1953], 1:99).

16. Cf. Raymond Wheeler, *The Laws of Human Nature: A General View of Gestalt Psychology* (New York: D. Appleton & Co., n.d.), pp. 129 ff., where the gestalt position that "the outstanding field property of any perceptual experience is its meaning" is set forth.

    By suggesting that the phenomenal world speaks to us in a language that we have largely given to it, I am not suggesting the necessity for some kind of "subjective idealism" (or "phenomenalism" that would hold that the recurring gestalt *is* the object: that any statement made about a material thing is exactly equivalent to a statement made about the gestalt). As I have tried to show earlier, insofar as the "subject" of experience exists, so does the "object"; perception, in other words, is within a subject/object framework. There is no knowledge of an object without the presence of the interpreting mind, and there is no knowledge without the presence of an objective form. Just as we can never know the empirical subject as it is apart from all its involvements with objects, so we can never know the empirical object apart from the interpretative processes by which we encounter it. There is no simple direct *cognitive* experience of an object as it is, upon which thought later supervenes, for a cognitive experience means precisely the activity of interpretation. Before the mind encounters (or superimposes itself upon) objects, they are by definition unknowable.

    My analysis then points neither to a "subjective idealism" which holds to the sole reality of the perceiving subject nor to an "objective realism" which holds to the independent reality of the perceived objects as they are in themselves. Within the structures of perception, there is both "subject" and "object," albeit, metaphysically the whole subject/object framework is an appearance to be transcended.

17. The term "monad" has been used by philosophers such as Nicolaus Cusanus (1401–1464), Bruno (1548–1600), and Leibniz (1646–1716) to signify basic metaphysical units or individuals that reflect the world in certain special ways. Cusanus defined a monad as any individual thing which mirrors the world, that is to say, looks upon it and forms its own representation of it. For Bruno, every monad is a microcosm,

it combines form and matter, spirit and body, and bears within itself a representation of all the basic principles of the universe. God (the *monas monadum*) contains all such principles in their original purity within himself. Leibniz, who developed this concept into a complete metaphysical position (a monadology), defined a monad as an unextended, indestructible, teleological substance. Each monad reflects the universe in a somewhat different way depending upon the clarity and intensity of its perception. And all monads are arranged, according to Leibniz, by a preordained harmony. For, "every substance expresses the whole sequence of the universe in accordance with its own viewpoint or relationship to the rest, so that all are in perfect correspondence with one another" (Leibniz to Hersen-Rheinfels, May 1686).

A kind of monadology is also present in the Indian system of Jainism, which elaborates the kinds of standpoints (*naya*) that a perceiver may take towards objects and the kinds of judgments which he may make—each of which must be qualified as "relatively" true (*syādvāda*). The doctrine emphasizes the pluralistic character of reality (*anekāntavāda*) and the fact that all perceptual knowing is necessarily limited to certain selected forms of experience. See, for example, the *Syādvādamañjarī*, a thirteenth-century commentary which presents the Jaina doctrines clearly and systematically.

18. One's attitudes, preconceptions, and expectations are clearly grounded to a considerable extent in social experience. We do not perceive atomically but socially, according to complex patterns of learning that are carried out in terms of group mores and values. There are different styles, as it were, of perception within different historical periods, and indeed within different age groups within a single period, and these styles go far to condition the individual's mode of perceiving. For example, among many young persons today throughout the world there is a style of perception, based on new electronic technology and expressed in new art forms, that looks for a projection or image of disparate forms simultaneously juxtaposed. Gestalts pass in and out of one another: they dissolve, overlap, reappear, etc., at a dazzling pace.

19. William James, *Psychology*, 2 vols. (New York: Henry Holt & Co., 1890), 1:289.

20. *Ibid.*

21. Jean Piaget, the distinguished child psychologist, writes that "originally the child puts the whole content of consciousness on the same plane and draws no distinction between the 'I' and the external world. ...the constitution of the idea of reality presupposes a progressive splitting-up of ... consciousness into two complementary universes—the objective universe and the subjective." (*The Child's Con-*

ception of Physical Causality, trans. Marjorie Gabain [Paterson, N.J.: Littlefield, Adams & Co., 1960], p. 242).

22. This is of course Aristotle's logic which most of us retain rather exclusively throughout our cognitive life: the logic, that is, which holds that the "laws of thought" (e.g., of excluded middle) are necessarily true of the external world.

HUMAN TELEOLOGY

1. The tendency to individualize need not, of course, result in a doctrine of "individualism" (economic, political, social)—which so often seems to mask a fixation on adolescent egoism and to be a disguised demand to exploit others—for it is possible to have real individuals in a social community. In fact the difference between a *community* of persons and a totalitarian organization of society (which is the natural enemy of the "individualist" and to which, at the same time, he seems to have a peculiar affinity) lies precisely in the community retaining to the fullest the quality of individual participation.

2. See *Beyond the Pleasure Principle*, chap. 5.

MAN'S TRANSCENDENTAL SELF

1. Traditional Indian (viz., Vedāntic) philosophy divides consciousness into four provinces, which are: (1) the waking state (*jāgarita-sthāna*) —our ordinary intentional awareness of an external world made up of material objects, events, and finite persons; (2) the dream or "subconscious" state (*svapna-sthāna*)—wherein, with the cessation of waking consciousness, we are involved with fancies, images and memories constituted and directed by various irrepressible instincts and drives; (3) the deep-sleep state (*suṣupti-sthāna*)—which is a kind of dreamless sleep of peace and well-being where all awareness of transient happenings is absent, and one is aware only of the fact of this absence; and (4) the state of absolute consciousness (*turīya*—literally, 'the fourth')—the state of unity where all duality and egoness is overcome. (See *Māṇḍūkya Upaniṣad*.)

   The "transcendental self" of man, as I seek to understand it here in its psychological dimension, is precisely this fourth state of consciousness identified by Vedānta. It is ego-less and impersonal; it is pure self-luminous consciousness.

2. This "unknowing knowing" is asserted in all traditions of spiritual experience, but it is perhaps brought out most clearly in the early Brahmanic tradition of India. In the *Kena Upaniṣad* (II. 3), for exam-

ple, it is stated: "To whomsoever it is not known, to him it is known: to whomsoever it is known, he does not know. It is not understood by those who understand it; it is understood by those who do not understand it." (Trans. S. Radhakrishnan)

3. St. Augustine's *ratio superior*, which enables man to recognize the "significance" of spiritual truth; Spinoza's *scientia intuitiva*, which grasps immediately the necessary connections in Nature so that the world is viewed *sub species aeternatitas* as it might view itself; Schelling's *intellektuelle Anschauung*, which penetrates directly into the indivisible unity of being; the *prajñā* of the Mādhyamika school of Buddhism which yields spiritual truth (*paramārtha*); the *jñāna* of the "way of knowledge" of Vedānta—are similar, in all essential respects, to the act of attaining "knowledge by identity." They all assert that the limits to man's noetic experience are self-imposed and are not essential. They all assert that man possesses the power to pursue a transcendental spiritual quest.

4. This does not mean, of course, that one cannot articulate various simple forms which, although they violate one or more of the usual requirements for thought when it is directed to the world of our ordinary experience, may justifiably be used when thought is directed toward the Absolute. The following forms would be instances of this:

(1) "Objective non-duality"—X is Y (or X is not-different from Y)—the essential identity of apparent dissimilarities, as expressed in the statement "Man is not-different from the Absolute."
(2) "Attribute similarity"—X is and is not Y—that something possesses both a given attribute and its negation, as expressed in the statement "The Absolute is at once personal and impersonal."
(3) "Mutual exclusion"—X is neither Y nor not-Y—something is neither one thing nor its opposite or contrary, as expressed in the statement "The Absolute is neither good nor evil (or not-good)."

These simple forms have no systematic relation with each other and by their very nature cannot be extended to the general domain of rational thought. They, and others like them, then, cannot form a "logic."

5. Even various Renaissance and early Post-Renaissance attempts to transform this logic (from its being an instrument of disputation to its being one of genuine discovery) were bound to its basic principles. See Peter Ramus (1515–1572), *Animadversions on Aristotle's Dialectic*.

6. Plato, who of course knew better than this and would have held that if there is nothing in the understanding which was not first in the senses then there is nothing of *value* in the understanding, was—as far as Greek logic was concerned—something of an anomaly. Plato himself, however, was very much dependent upon the laws of thought as

formalized by Aristotle. A great number of the problems raised by Socrates in the dialogues, and the inability of his protagonists to deal with them satisfactorily, are based directly on these laws (e.g., the "proofs" for the immortality of the soul in the *Phaedo*).

7. It is interesting to observe the extent to which Bertrand Russell, one of the most important figures in modern logic, remains tied to Aristotle. In his *Philosophy of Logical Atomism*, published in 1918, Russell gives the impression that he arrives at a metaphysics by way of his logic. The reverse, however, is the case. His logic is quite clearly based on a metaphysical position which in certain fundamentals is not significantly different from that of Aristotle. Russell himself states: "When I say that my logic is atomistic, I mean that I share the common-sense belief that there are many separate things." And, "the first truism ... is that the world contains facts which are what they are whatever we may choose to think about them and that there are also beliefs which have reference to facts, and by reference to facts are either true or false." And, "...if one goes into what I call Logical Atomism that means that one does believe the world can be analyzed into a number of separate things with relations and so forth...." (*Philosophy of Logical Atomism*, I, II)

8. Cf. *Popular Science Monthly*, 1878. In the case of pragmatism we do not have so much a *formal logic* of thought as we do a *theory of truth*, and later with Dewey a *method of inquiry*. We deal with pragmatism here mainly because of its articulation of certain pervasive traits of our ordinary thought processes and because, as with Aristotelian and Hegelian logic, we get into many difficulties when we transfer the pragmatic "attitude" or "method" to reality.

9. James also demands a certain "coherence" of ideas. In speaking approvingly of the instrumental theory of Dewey and Schiller he states *"that ideas ... become true just in so far as they help us to get into satisfactory relation with other parts of our experience ...."* And that a new idea which is adopted as true "preserves the older stock of truths with a minimum of modification, stretching them just enough to make them admit the novelty.... New-truth is always a go-between, a smoother-over of transitions. It marries old opinion to new fact so as ever to show a minimum of jolt, a maximum of continuity. We hold a theory true just in proportion to its success in solving this 'problem of maxima and minima'." *Pragmatism* (New York: Longmans, Green & Co., 1949), pp. 58, 60–61.

10. John Dewey, *Logic and the Theory of Inquiry* (New York: Henry Holt & Co., 1938), pp. 3–4. Cf. *ibid.*, p. 5, for his definition of "warranted assertibility."

Dewey preferred to call himself an "instrumentalist" rather than a "pragmatist," in order, perhaps, to dissociate himself from William James, the more brilliant expositor of pragmatism.

11. *Ibid.*, p. 66.

12. It is possible to add two other modern attempts to resolve the problem of the relation between thought and reality: the attempts made by the schools of "symbolic logic" and by Existentialism. It was discovered in the nineteenth century, primarily by mathematicians (e.g., Karl F. Gauss, Herman Minkowski, G. F. B. Rienmann), that the fundamental premises of geometry were largely "arbitrary." Euclidian geometry, which, like Aristotelian logic, reigned without serious critical appraisal for hundreds of years, was seen to involve premises which were theoretically unnecessary: one could deduce geometric theorems from other premises and, in fact, one could construct a perfectly coherent and cogent system of geometry from radically different premises. This discovery was of immense importance, for it was also soon discovered that the new systems of non-euclidian geometry could have an important place in the physical sciences (e.g., quantum physics). In philosophy proper these discoveries led to a complete reinvestigation of the logical foundations of mathematics, and to the foundations of logic itself. It was demonstrated (e.g., by Bertrand Russell and A. N. Whitehead in *Principia Mathematica*, 1910–1913) that the basic structure of mathematics could be derived from certain elementary logical relations. With this accomplished, the next step was to create various new logics and logistic systems and to hold that logic could exist independent of all questions of ontology. It could be a kind of pure theoretic science in its own right. Whereas pragmatism sought to establish the relations between logic and reality by limiting the notion of reality to the empirical and the practical (and forging its logical tools accordingly), the new schools of logic seek to resolve the problem by denying it. Whatever reality might be, logic can be independent of it. According to Existentialism, on the other hand, which is the philosophy of living problems par excellence, truth is essentially subjective—a quality of the thinker rather than simply of the thought. Existentialism has not come forward, however, with a "logic" of subjectivity, of existential thought —and it is indeed incapable of doing so. Existentialism (at least of the Sartrean variety) would disappear if it had a "logic," for it asserts the basic "irrationality" of reality.

MAN'S RELATION TO THE DIVINE

1. *Ascent of Mount Carmel*, trans. E. Allison Peers (New York: Doubleday & Co., Image Books, n.d.), Prologue, p. 14.

Index

Absolute: definition of, 6; identical with Self, 6; inexpressibility of, 7; task of philosophy in relation to, 9; as creative-being, 15–18; as being, 35 *passim;* as valuable-being, 89–90; as content of experience, 90 *passim*
Alexander, Samuel, 118n6
Aquinas, St. Thomas, 42
Aristotle: his definition of soul, 19; his conception of categories, 36; and laws of logic, 95–96; and the perception of time, 131–132n22
Augustine, St.: and sinful man, 30–31; his analysis of time, 133–134n26

Beauty, 89
Bergson, Henri: nature of metaphysics, ix; and intuition, 24; idea of continuity, 50; and memory, 129n10
Buddhism: view of the self, 102n2; and doctrine of will, 188–119n7

Cassirer, Ernst, 73, 143n15
Categories: interpretations of, 36–37; metaphysical status of, 37–39 *passim*; table of, 40; of feeling, 41–44; of mind, 44–51; of understanding, 51–60; Hegelian view of, 127n2
Causality: as a category of understanding, 58–59; limits of application, 121–122n14; Leibniz, Kant, Hume on, 135–136n31; in early Western and in Asian thought, 136–137n33
Chinese Philosophy: idea of rhythm, 127–128n1; and integrity, 128n5;

doctrine of *jen*, 130–131n15; and causality, 137n33
Christianity, 27, 30–32
Communication, 125–126n11. *See also* Existentialism
Consciousness: Sartre's view of, 28–29; and space-time, 53; transcendental form of, 91–93; waking form of, 92 *passim*; Vedāntic view of, 146n1
Consistency, 50–51
Continuity, 50–51
Creativity: of the Divine, 16 *passim*; and conditioning, 17; as illusory, 17; Upaniṣadic view of, 120–121n9; Spinoza's doctrine of, 122n15

Detachment, 106
Dewey, John, 98, 99
Dualism, 79 *passim*

Enlightenment, ix
Equilibrium, 48–49
Existentialism: its view of man, 27; and self-understanding, 29; and logic; 148n12

Faith, 106–107
Fear, 64
Feuerbach, Ludwig, 31
Fichte, Johann, 55, 119n7
Freud, Sigmund: and the death instinct, 83; and spiritual love, 117n4; and the aggressive instinct, 139–140n5; and the superego, 140n6